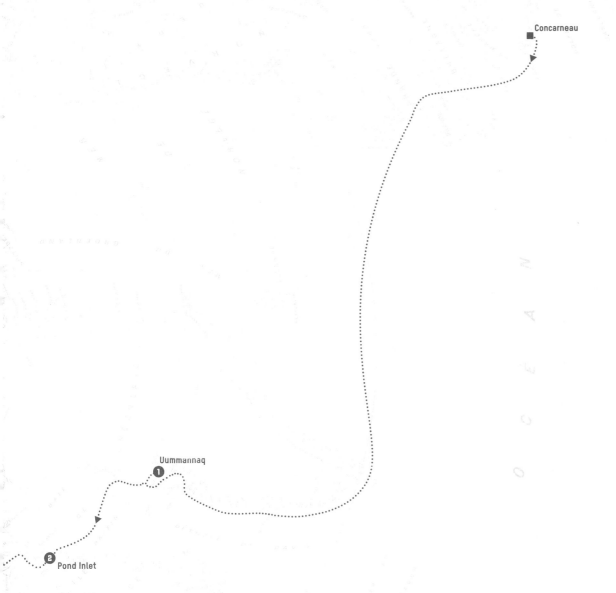

Concarneau

Uummannaq
①

② Pond Inlet

Gjoa Haven

OCEAN

NORD

ATLANTIQUE

Emmanuelle Périé-Bardout   Ghislain Bardout   PHOTOS Franck Gazzola

BETWEEN TWO WORLDS

FORWORD François Gabart and Virginie Valentini-Gabart

UNDER THE POLE III
Four years of deep diving
for scientific exploration

UNDER
THE POLE
UNDERWATER SCIENTIFIC EXPLORATION

ulmer

Credits

All photographs by Franck Gazzola,
except for:

Beau Pilgrim : portrait of F. Gazzola (jacket).
Ghislain Bardout : pp. 94, 112 h g, 116 b g, 118 (2),
130, 131, 132, 152-153, 176-177, 179 h, 180-181.
Aldo Ferrucci : pp. 136-137, 172.
Alexis Courcoux : p. 5.
Maxime Horlaville : pp. 65, 100-101, 102, 104
d, 106-107, 118 (2), 119 (8), 141, 146-147, 150-151,
156, 160, 161, 163, 164, 165, 166-167, 168, 169, 170,
171, 174-175.
Gaël Lagarrigue : pp. 12-13, 15, 16 m, 16 b, 17, 18, 19,
20, 21, 23 h d, 24-25, 26, 26-27, 45 b d, 52-53, 55, 62h
g, 62 b g, 67, 88, 89, 92, 93, 95, 96, 97, 142 h g.
Julien Leblond : pp. 90-91, 112-113, 144-145, 181 d.
Quentin Mateus : p. 199.
Alec Magnan : pp. 182, 183, 184-185.
Erwan Marivint : pp. 115, 118 (1), 125, 134-135, 144 h
g, 157, 158 g, 187.
Philippe Mura - Les Compagnons du Saga : p. 195.
Nicolas Paulme : p. 142 b.
Emmanuelle Périé-Bardout : pp. 119 (12), 179 b.
Kevin Peyrusse : pp. 50-51.
Yann Poupart : p. 237 (5).
Benoît Poyelle : p. 46.
Marta Sostres : pp. 10-11, 14, 16 h, 68-69 b.
Thomas Trapier : pp. 202 b g, 208-209, 209 d, 214,
222, 224, 226 b, 226-227, 236-237 (sauf 5 & 11).

Maps (endpapers, pp. 6-7) : © Shom

For Robin and Tom; thank you for sharing
our dreams while also dreaming your own.

**This book was manufactured
in an eco-friendly way.**

The pages (Gardamatt art® 170gsm) and
cover (Gardamatt art® 150gsm) are made
with a minimum of 70% of FSC certified
fibre from sustainably managed forests.

This book was printed in Italy by Printer
Trento using vegetable inks. For 20 years
we have been working with these printers
who aim to adopt the most ecologically
responsible production methods possible.

© 2021 Les Éditions Ulmer
33, rue du Faubourg Montmartre
75009 Paris
Tél. : 01 48 05 03 03
www.editions-ulmer.fr

Design: Guillaume Duprat
Editor in Chief: Antoine Isambert
Editorial Production Manager: Raphaèle Dorniol
Translation: Simon Garbutt
Printing: Printer Trento, srl
ISBN: 978-2-37922-231-3
Edition N°: 231-01

Find us on Facebook and Instagram

Legal deposit: October 2021
Printed in Italy

FOREWORD
BY FRANÇOIS GABART AND VIRGINIE VALENTINI-GABART

As their "pontoon neighbours" (when Emmanuelle and Ghislain are not off to the other side of the world on an expedition), we have always had great admiration and respect for this inspiring couple, who had the courage to leave for the polar zones with two young children, to explore the ocean floor and bear witness to its richness and fragility.

Although our paths have often crossed in Concarneau, we have never had the chance to talk at length about our respective passions and our common love for the ocean. So it was without really knowing them well, yet feeling that we share many mutual connections, that we followed their earlier adventures in the ice and now the enthralling account of their third expedition, Under The Pole III. We have been fascinated by the numerous dives and associated discoveries, impressed by the team's coolheadness, amazed by the breathtaking landscapes, and moved by the human relationships and shared values that shine through these adventures.

As ocean racing enthusiasts ourselves, the surface of the water is our playground; our knowledge of the deep sea is limited. Yet it is in these deep, dark waters, so little known, that the future of the planet may be played out. The ocean plays a fundamental role in the balance of the Earth and its living beings. Whether we live on the coast or thousands of kilometres away from it, we all breathe the oxygen that the ocean produces. Marine biodiversity is dangerously impacted by human activity. We all have a responsibility and a role to play in reversing this trend.

While this book is a valuable mine of information, we were also sensitive to the significance that Emmanuelle and Ghislain wished to give to their project: to invent, to innovate... yes, but to push back the frontiers of knowledge and the limits of Mankind, in sharing knowledge and respect for the environment, and to respond to the ecological and societal challenges of our century! These aspirations echo our own desire to move towards making ocean racing more environmentally friendly and to contribute to the development of sustainable maritime mobility.

Fascinating, inspiring, instructive and moving, this book also introduces us to some generous, humble, supportive people who respect their environment: a real message of hope! Although it may not completely cure the ills of our world, Emmanuelle and Ghislain's reassuring account makes us want to fight for our planet and our children. We owe them our thanks.

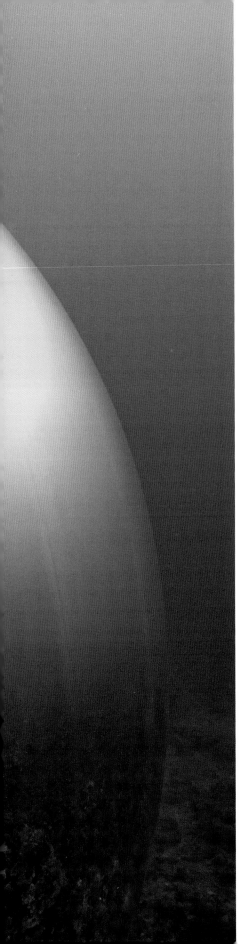

BETWEEN TWO WORLDS

There are places everywhere that human beings manage to reach where they are able to spend enough time to glimpse a different world but not long enough to understand it. This is how exploration begins, as a quest to answer our questions. In fact, exploration is infinite, universal and timeless. We can always look a little further, look closer, rethink what we thought we knew.

The same is true of how we look at the oceans and the creatures that inhabit them. Except that, more so than anywhere else, the oceans retain an unfathomable degree of mystery. Like space. They are so big, so deep... What do we know about them? Can we only begin to understand them? This is how Under The Pole was born, in 2008. We were a young couple who shared a passion for the polar regions, diving and sailing. We were curious... and full of fight. With sea ice melting ever faster, the first UTP expedition set out in 2010 to document the hidden face of the pack ice in the heart of the frozen Arctic Ocean. The success of this difficult, extreme expedition encouraged us to continue further down the path of undersea exploration. It would be three years until, in January 2014, we set sail on our schooner, the WHY, for our second expedition. For two years we dived in Greenland after the sea ice had retreated in spring, letting ourselves be imprisoned by it in the winter in between. Following the rhythm of the seasons, and during our meetings with the Greenlanders, we took the time to make discoveries. When we returned home, at the end of 2015, we laid the groundwork for the third expedition, described in this book.

More than ever before, in a global context of collapsing biodiversity and the climate emergency, we wanted scientific research to be at the heart of this new chapter. Our dreams of exploration still survived, with each of these ends naturally complementing the other.

During all these years we have sometimes felt that we were walking a tightrope, trying to find our balance. On a personal level, it meant finding a balance between continuing to accomplish our ambitions while at the same time starting a family; on the ground, when the pack ice, so beautiful one day, was ready to break up the next; beneath those same ice floes, which are at the edge of the world and yet badly affected by pollution; in the villages we visited, in the Arctic and Polynesia, where people are trying to preserve their cultural identity that is under threat from the excesses of Westernisation; between the surface and the depths, where each incursion is a journey; and between life on land and in the ocean, where we dreamt of staying.

A diver, in essence, moves between two worlds. But as he sinks into the depths and spends time there, he perceives that it is in fact the sum of two worlds. Parallel universes, like a millefeuille, each having their own differences, their enigmas, governed by their own rules, but which nevertheless meet and sometimes interact. There is not a single dive when we don't take a last look back at the depths before ascending, wondering what is still hidden there. Or what will play out there once we have left this place that has opened its doors to us but which we can only explore on borrowed time. Because mankind always encounters two limits in his quest for knowledge of the undersea environment: depth and time. To come up against them is to face our own limits.

For four years, during this third Under The Pole expedition, we have got to know these boundaries, exploring them so as to be able to move gently between two worlds at last. And to remember that they are in fact a single world of which we are but a part, and which we must fight fiercely to protect.

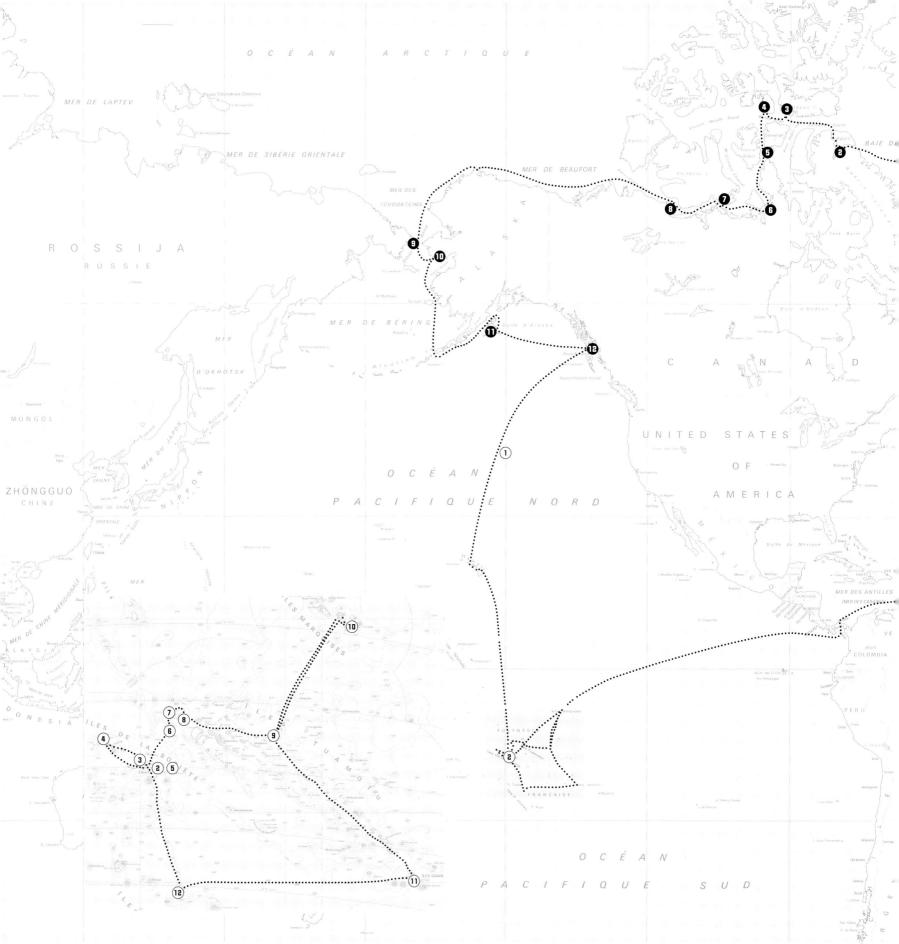

NORTH-WEST PASSAGE

PASSAGE

LIGHT
BENEATH THE ARCTIC

A homecoming of sorts for Robin, who had his third birthday in Uummannaq Bay and lived there for 18 months.

RETURN
TO GREENLAND

6ᵗʰ July 2017, arrival at Uummannaq

The sea we encounter for this first voyage is wild and bad-tempered. Never mind, we are happy to be on board. Robin and Tom are resilient sailors. I'm not worried; we feel more at home on board the WHY than anywhere else in the last few years. Seeing the heart-shaped mountain[1] appear in front of the bow I feel as though I'm coming home. I am deeply moved, because this small community holds so many memories for us. By morning the sea is calm and we glide forward under sail, surrounded by icebergs glittering in the sun. Tom points at the mountains and the sea. Robin asks: 'Is Uummannaq over there?'... What does he remember about our adventure two years ago? Already a familiar red motor launch is approaching. Our friends Paaluk, Ann-Mette and their daughter Evona climb on board the WHY to accompany us to Uummannaq. Still in shock, they tell us – while the three children happily climb on the dodger[2] – how only a few days earlier a tsunami had devastated two villages on the bay, killing four

people including a very young child. The 250 evacuated inhabitants have been temporarily rehoused in Uummannaq's sports hall and boarding school. Experience and the rigours of High-Arctic life have turned Greenlanders into a very close-knit, supportive community, who have organized collections of clothing, toys and money. Paaluk says that on their way to meet us they had spotted some Greenland right whales, a rare sight both at this time of year and here in the bay. We anchor in the port where we will stay for several days, preparing our diving kit, deciding on the sites for our research and enjoying catching up with our friends.

1   Uummannaq means "heart-shaped mountain" in Greenlandic.
2   The dodger is the shelter surrounding the helm on the bridge.

Uummannaq means "heart-shaped" in Greenlandic, because of the shape of this impressive mountain overlooking the village. In this small West Greenland community, memories are still scarred by the recent tsunami, caused by a landslide south of the Umiammakku Nunaat peninsula.

11th July, first dives

The water in Spraglebugten Bay is so clear that we can see right to the bottom. We are getting ready to dive with Marcel Koken in search of bioluminescent life forms. At around 10m (33ft) below the surface I meet Ghislain, filming with Kevin. Two angel sharks are mating without seeming in the least disturbed by our presence. For several minutes we witness this pure, poetic spectacle in waters that are among the most hostile in the world. Angel sharks have fascinated me ever since I first met them beneath the underside of the North Pole. I watch Marcel rummaging through the kelp and collecting samples. He shows me some algal encrustations that change colour under the beam of his torch. He seems to know exactly where to look and spends a long time on a single square metre, stirring up so much sediment that eventually we are left completely in the dark!

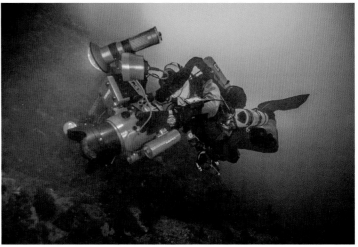

At the end of the day we visit "Santa Claus's Castle", a traditional turf building, still intact, where a Danish film crew lived for several years. We make sure to write our Christmas letters in the guest book at the entrance... lots of trains and tractors for Robin, clear water and cetaceans for me! But the most precious gift is right in front of our eyes: the view of the ice-filled bay, the green grass under our feet and the flowing stream, foxes playing around and the wild flowers under the sunlit slopes of Mount Uummannaq. Nature's magic surpasses anything in a child's fairytale.

Top left: First dive in search of fluorescence against the backdrop of Spraglebugten Bay and "Santa Claus's Castle".

Centre left: Kevin Peyrusse films with his camera fitted with ultraviolet lights to spot traces of fluorescence. This phenomenon exists on all types of living organisms: fish, crustaceans, larvae, algae...

Bottom left: Cyril unfolds the quadrat (a frame 40cm [15.7in] square) and samples everything inside. This standardized method makes it possible to make an inventory of the biodiversity in the areas visited.

Contrary to what is sometimes believed about the Arctic seabed, it is very diverse depending on the region, the depth and the season. Here, the sea floor is particularly rich, covered with sponges, soft corals and anemones.

While watching whales in the low light of the midnight sun, we are surprised to see Jorut and Joana coming towards us. We met them while wintering the WHY in Ikerasak Bay in 2015, and made strong bonds of friendship. They had spent several days in Disko Bay trying to repair the engine of their skiff so that they could return and meet up with us before we left for the Northwest Passage

There is a lot of emotion in our eyes and we have much to talk about! Emmanuelle and Véronique learned to speak a little Greenlandic during the previous expedition. This is enough, with gestures and looks, to tell each other about the last year.

Every evening, we invite Jorut and Joana for a meal in the WHY's saloon, at anchor in Ikerasak. On our last evening, Paaluk, Ann-Mette, Arnatsiaq, and Jens join us to celebrate our departure.

The night of 23rd July

In low, raking, midnight light, the WHY manoeuvres between exhaling whales on its way to Ikerasak. A small skiff draws our attention away from the giants. At the same time I get a premonition. Ghislain first spots one person through her binoculars, then confirms what I was already thinking: "It's Jorut and Joanna!" In their fragile craft Joanna raises both arms and shouts "Ahoy! Tikilluaritsi!"[3] We greet each other with the same feelings and warmth as when we said goodbye two years earlier; it is as if we had never parted. We made firm bonds then, while overwintering the WHY, and are enormously fond of each other. On the bridge they bring us up to date with the last few months' news: the seal hunt, which was poor this year (just one!), the four reindeer they hunted at Nussuaq that filled the freezer, and the whale that was shared by the whole village. In a few months their son Frederik will become father to a little boy. They still don't know whether to stay at Ikerasak or whether they'll go to Nuuk, where Frederik's in-laws live. I can't imagine them leaving their little village to go to the capital. Jorut has always hunted and fished, he lives out on the ice with his dogs and loves this simple life, close to nature. In 2013, Jorut took me with him and his dogs to hunt seal at the far end of the bay: four days at -30°C to -40°C, an average of 14 hours a day on the sled, lots of coffee and tea, and at last a seal, shared between the dogs and the couple's own food store. I may be a vegetarian nowadays but I understand the justification for hunting in Greenland. Mammals, birds and fish are unique resources in the north of the country. Eaten raw, they are also the only source of vitamins. Nothing grows there, everything else is imported. Hunting is basically for survival, a subsistence hunt practised with respect for the animals, taking from nature only what is needed. Nothing is wasted here.

We spend two days at Ikerasak. They pass quickly but allow us time to discuss, in my stumbling Greenlandic and their similarly approximate English, our plans and our forthcoming itinerary in the Northwest Passage. The last dinner with our friends on board the WHY is filled with warmth and laughter, as well as a few tears when we weigh anchor. When will we see each other again? Greenland's flag flutters in the window of the little blue house. It may have been exploration that first brought us to Greenland but above all it is the Inuit[4] – in the literal sense – who draw us inexorably back again.

3 "Hello! Welcome!"

4 Inuit means "the people" in Greenlandic.

POND INLET,
IN THE ICE AND MIST

28th July, crossing

Upernavik isn't my favourite port in Greenland. Perhaps because of its quay, which wrecks boats, or the harbour itself, exposed to the winds and sea, or, this time, the dead dog floating just under the surface of the water. We only stay long enough to drop off Vincent at the airport, stock up with provisions and do a safety briefing in case we ever have to evacuate the WHY. We have laboriously downloaded a weather forecast that predicts a moderate wind, easing off for our arrival in the icy zone. We decide to set off, as the trend of the last few days indicates a good chance that the ice will break up at the entrance to Pond Inlet fjord. Beneath a radiant sun we watch Greenland's coast and majestic mountains recede as we head under full sail between giant icebergs and inquisitive seals. Quickly the wind picks up and waves toss the hull, cruelly testing our stomachs. As the weather gets even worse – we remind ourselves that forecasts are only relatively reliable here – we start worrying about the conditions we might encounter in the ice zone, the challenge being not to get trapped in pack ice. We manage to get a new weather forecast that matches our current conditions more closely. Finally, after four days at sea, the wind drops to nothing and the sea becomes a lake. We struggle to get through the icy

minefield, taking turns in the crow's nest to find a way through the drifting ice floes that block our passage. After several hours of this "game", we reach open water just as a thick fog envelops us. The barometer falls abruptly, indicating that a serious gale is imminent. Fog, sea ice, cold, damp... Ghislain and I search wildly for the shore while drinking litres of coffee. Early in the morning we enter the fjord, relieved to have found shelter at last, while watching the wind rise to more than 30 knots ($34\frac{1}{2}$ mph), confirming the barometer reading.

31st July, arrival

It is July 31st and the grey sky and black cliffs falling sheer into a frozen sea have left me thoughtful, wavering between relief at having arrived and happiness at having completed a treacherous voyage. Suddenly, combining crossing the Northwest Passage with diving for scientific research seems extremely ambitious to me. But the sun returns, throwing a mysterious light onto the fjord, warming my chilly bones, washing away my doubts, and through the clearing mist Pond Inlet appears before our eyes.

Reaching the Canadian coast comes as a relief after a journey marked by strong winds, ice and fog. Sleep deprivation kicks in after two nights spent picking our way while watching out for ice.

Pond Inlet on Baffin Island is our gateway to Canada. This is where we pick up our friend "Bilou" (the sailor Roland Jourdain), Isabelle, Franck (the team photographer) and Kayak, whom it was easier to collect here. The team is complete, but really overstaffed: there are 17 of us on board for the next three weeks!

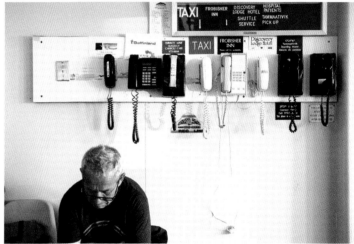

Above, top: Pond Inlet has about 1,500 inhabitants. Its waters are ice-free for an average of three and a half months a year.

Above: Bilou at the airport.
Uber doesn't seem to have made it here yet.

While we are celebrating our arrival in Pond Inlet's small restaurant, we are evicted from the village by... pack ice. We weigh anchor at one in the morning to head for the anchorage of Albert Harbour several miles away. A very mediocre anchorage, it must be said in passing. But when we decide to dive there, the site turns out to be one of the most beautiful we have ever known in the Arctic: a wall plunging to a depth of more than 80m (260ft), with exceptional visibility and plenty of life. A strong surface current makes entering the water and the recovery of divers rather... rock and roll. I dive to do the lighting for Kevin who is filming Ghislain and Cyril taking samples from the wall. The cold grips my hands almost immediately. Throughout the dive I shift between pain and wonderment. Cyril and I return to the surface while Ghislain and Kevin, wearing rebreathers, are still waiting at the decompression stage, compensating for the time that they had spent at depth before we reached them. The current forces us to take refuge on the shingle before Erwan picks us up on the semi-inflatable rescue boat. We freeze when we see the warning system appear on the parachute, triggering the safety procedure. Kevin had a water leak in his glove and was getting shocks in his arm from the electric heating system in his clothing under his dry suit. Water and electricity are not good partners! Everything is back to normal when he turns off the heating system, with the added bonus of having provided a safety drill for the surface team. We fill up our water supplies at a waterfall and also have a wash "at the source" before leaving to pick up Bilou[5], Isabelle, Franck and Kayak from the airport. Kayak jumps on us, licking every face within reach and making little Tom laugh; the crew is now complete.

5   Bilou is the nickname of yachtsman Roland Jourdain.

Filling the WHY's tanks "at source"
in Albert Harbour, which also gave us
some of our most beautiful Arctic dives.

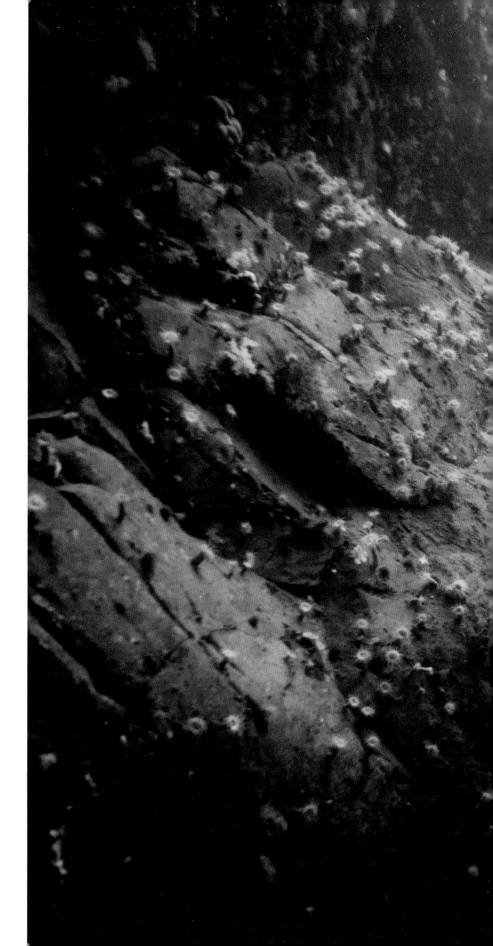

Above, top: Carrying out a biodiversity inventory and fluorescence research with the quadrat.

Above: The walls of the drop-off are covered with a rich, colourful flora despite the depth. There is also quite a rich fauna, even though we do not encounter any Greenland sharks, which we had been able to observe several times in the north of Greenland in 2014.

Opposite: Albert Harbour marks the start of our Northwest Passage diving campaign. The currents are strong at the surface and the site is vertical, which makes the diving technical, but the clear water and magnificent undersea cliff face are an invitation to deep diving.

BEECHEY ISLAND,
STEPPING BACK
INTO POND INLET'S HISTORY

3th August, departure from Pond Inlet

Our departure from Pond Inlet marks the start of our voyage through the Passage. At the map table with Ghislain we measure yet again the immense distances to be covered, with many miles between each scheduled stopover. Frustratingly we pass a bay famous for its population of narwhals, but we must take advantage of the fair weather to move on. The sea is what surfers call "glassy": flat, without a wrinkle on its surface, a perfect mirror. For the first time Robin climbs to the top of the mast with Ghislain as we pass our last large icebergs. He hangs there fearlessly. Tom crawls happily across the bridge, looking like he wants to follow them even though he can't walk yet. We stop near a large ice floe where about thirty seals are basking.

As we move onward the landscape becomes austere, the sky leaden. Like a ghost of past expeditions, the WHY, still under sail, slices through the mist. We are in Lancaster Sound. Now I understand better a few lines that Amundsen wrote on arriving at the same spot, and which he seems to be whispering to me: "the North Devon coast that we are following does not have Greenland's beautiful lines; heavy, massive plateaus, bare and desolate, humped here and there with large rocky protuberances. This country is not appealing!" No, not appealing, yet I find these landscapes have an almost incomprehensible attraction for me; it feels as though time has no influence here.

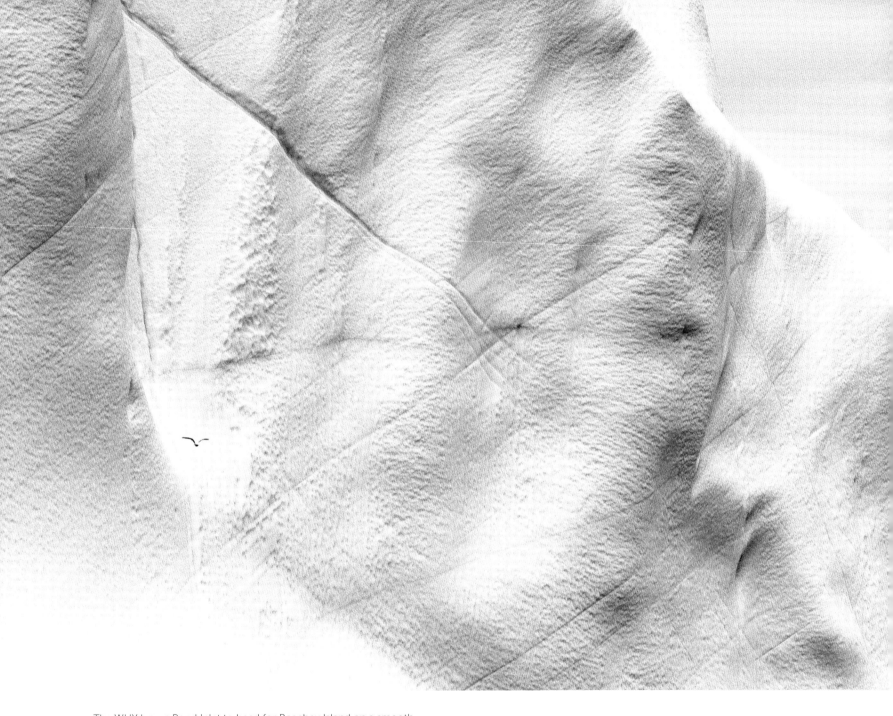

The WHY leaves Pond Inlet to head for Beechey Island on a smooth
sea that reflects the sky, icebergs and mountains. We pass several large
icebergs, their blue hues illuminating a raw, dark landscape. They will
be the last we see in this region because we will be too far from the
glaciers where they are calved.

Previous double-page spread: The hostility of this place is matched only by its beauty. The ocean reflects this iceberg perfectly, like a Rorschach test before our fascinated eyes.

Above, top: Robin comes down from the mast where he has just spent over an hour contemplating the landscape.

Above: Tom, 13 months old as we set out, is the WHY's youngest crew member. He will take his first steps on board in the Northwest Passage.

Opposite: Here, the WHY shows the scale of the icebergs that cross our path. It is in this magnificent setting that Robin, aged 5, first climbs the mast, accompanied by Ghislain. Unaffected by vertigo, it will be the first of many such ascents for him.

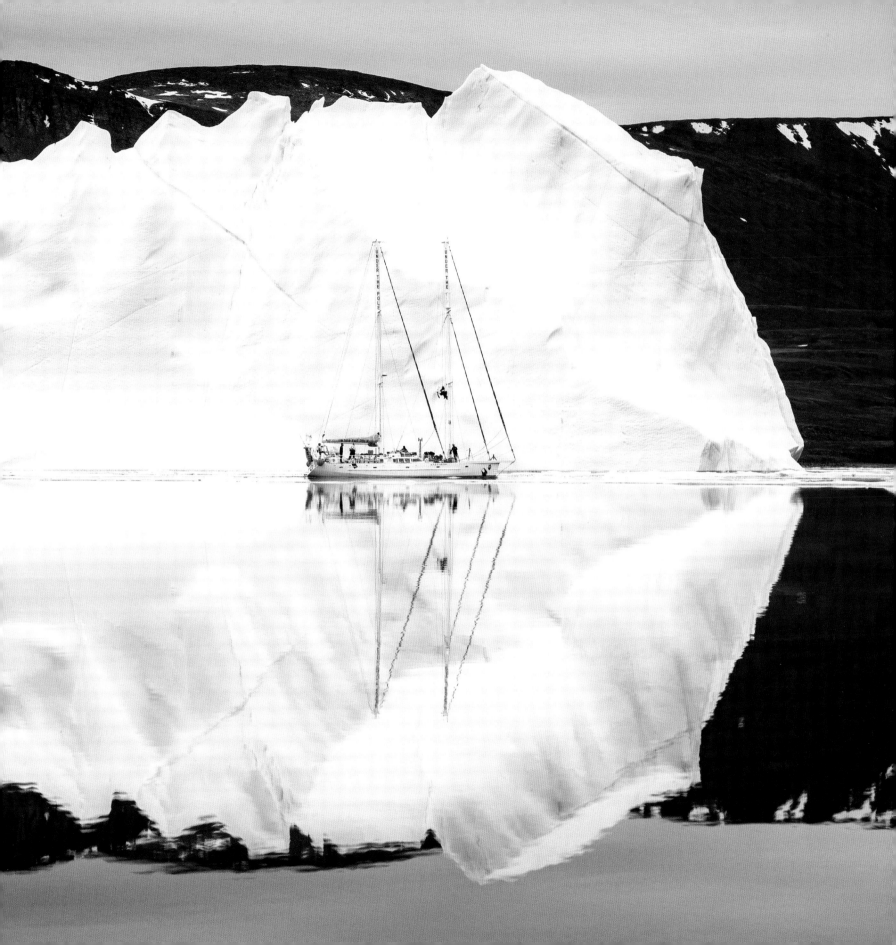

A flight of eider ducks skims over the sea
in front of the mountains and black cliffs
typical of this region.

Boats rarely cross this isolated region. A bearded seal watches us curiously. The name comes from the whiskers they use on the seabed to detect their prey, mainly cephalopods, cod, molluscs, shrimps and crabs. Its main predators in the wild are polar bears and killer whales.

Next double-page spread: The WHY, its sails goose-winged, passes bare cliffs that seem to disappear into a grey ceiling. Approaching Beechey Island, the atmosphere is hostile, almost mystical.

Beechey Island has left its mark on the history of the Passage, in particular the tragic shipwrecks of HMS Terror and HMS Erebus from Franklin's expedition. In 1845 Sir John Franklin, a seasoned expedition leader, mounted an ambitious expedition to force a passage in the Northwest. By the standards of his time he was well equipped for success: two strong vessels – the Erebus and the Terror – built to withstand the pressure of the ice, a crew of 138 men and substantial provisions in newly designed cans. Yet after three years with no news, it was obvious that the expedition had been lost with all hands. Lady Jane, Franklin's widow, ceaselessly organized search parties. About 40 ships set out to hunt for them, often losing lives and vessels in their turn. At last it was McClintock, a well-organized captain, passionate about the polar world, who penetrated some of the mystery surrounding the shipwrecks. After two over-winterings, one of them halfway between Melville Bay and Baffin Island, he returned with precious information gathered principally from the oral tradition of local Inuit or the messages left in cairns[6] by the crew themselves, saying that they had left their ships and telling of the death of Franklin and a party of his men.

On Beechey Island, not far from the monument to Bellot[7], McClintock set up a marble tablet sent by Lady Jane in memory of Franklin's crew.

6   A pile of stones built by polar explorers or alpine climbers to show where they have been. Messages can also be left in them.
7   Joseph-René Bellot was a French naval officer and explorer, born 18th March 1826 in Paris, who died on the 18th August 1853 near Devon Island, in the Canadian Archipelago, now called Nunavut (Canada), while searching for the Franklin expedition.

Beechey Island is a landmark in the history of the Northwest Passage. Headstones and ruined makeshift barracks are the visible signs of the tragedies that took place here. Everything about this place reminds us of the challenge of navigation in these regions, even today and despite technical progress.

So today, at one end of the site, you find Bellot's memorial and the tablet dedicated to Franklin, as well as the remains of barracks and, at the far end of the beach, a line of four graves. Here lie three young crewmen who did not survive the first winter and one man who died during the search campaigns. It is hard not to be deeply moved in thinking of their tragic destinies. Their story will stay with us throughout the Passage, a necessary reminder of the dangers of navigating these waters. More than 170 years may have passed but vigilance and humility are still essential.

At the end of the afternoon, most of our crew come ashore for a hike that takes us to Franklin's cairn. It is a magnificent walk in a lunar landscape. The view is awe-inspiring. On our return we stand facing the WHY and admire what is, and will always remain, one of its most beautiful arctic anchorages. If only we could ignore the temperature and take away the ice surrounding us, we could believe ourselves to be in a tropical lagoon with emerald waters.

Above left: The marble memorial in memory of Franklin and his crew stands near the place where they tried to survive their first winter.

Centre left: A plaque in honour of Joseph-René Bellot, who took part in a rescue mission, financed by Lady Franklin, that led the French officer to his death.

Left: Memorial to John Torrington, a young crew member of HMS Terror, who died tragically at the age of 19.

In the middle of the Arctic summer one can only imagine how hostile this desolate, lunar landscape must have been when the explorers had to plan how to get their crews through the winter.

Left: Group photo on the cairn at the island's highest point, littered with barrel hoops and other remnants of the missions that were stranded on the island.

Above, top: Hikes are always a welcome way to stretch the legs after several days of sailing.

Above: We are in polar bear territory. Training with real bullets and flares is essential to stay calm in case of meeting one. If you are well prepared, you can almost always avoid a fatal outcome.

NATURAL FLUORESCENCE & BIOLUMINESCENCE IN THE ARCTIC

DR MARCEL KOKEN
LABOCEA-CNRS
(National Centre for Scientific Research)

The jellyfish *Aequorea victoria* is a species well known to scientists because it led to the discovery of "GFP" (Green Fluorescent Protein), which has important uses as a marker in biology and medicine.

Natural fluorescence and bioluminescence are two light phenomena used by underwater flora and fauna. The emission of light is essential for many functions such as communication, predation or defence.

Fluorescence is a physical phenomenon that transforms one colour of light into another, for example a fluorescent strip on a safety vest. As for bioluminescence, it is light emitted directly by a living organism via a chemical reaction, such as that produced by a glow-worm.

As a marine biologist at the CNRS, specializing in natural fluorescence and bioluminescence, my work involves isolating and typifying proteins involved in these phenomena. This type of protein is of great interest in many fields and has many applications, such as the green fluorescent protein isolated from a jellyfish, *Aequorea victoria*, which can be used, for example, to mark and track cancer cells.

The Under The Pole III expedition enabled scientific exploration, never previously undertaken, of the fluorescent and bioluminescent capabilities of underwater organisms in the Arctic, including the mesophotic zone. The polar regions have the peculiarity of alternating between six months of permanent daylight and six months of polar night.

This light regime is ideal for testing the following hypotheses:
- Because sunlight is needed to excite fluorescent molecules, if the sun is absent for six months, few arctic underwater organisms will exhibit fluorescent patterns.
- Conversely, having several months of "night", the polar environment promotes bioluminescence, produced independently of sunlight.

To test out these hypotheses, I sailed on board UTP's schooner from Uummannaq in Greenland to Kodiak, Alaska between July and October 2017, discovering underwater organisms with fluorescent and bioluminescent properties. In the laboratory, we have ultra-sensitive luminometers, spectro-fluorimeters and cameras to detect these phenomena. As this equipment cannot be submerged, we have had to adapt the divers' equipment

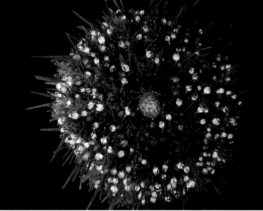

In order to identify the species and better understand the role of these light phenomena, some individual specimens were brought back on board the WHY to be tested in a dark room. In all, more than 100 different species were analysed in this way.

The results revealed a limited number (less than 10%) of fluorescent species in the polar environment compared with tropical and temperate ecosystems (about 20 to 30%), which are brightly lit all year round. These data support the initial hypothesis suggesting that the absence of sunlight limits the use of natural fluorescence by polar species for signalling. Bioluminescence was observed towards the end of the expedition, coinciding with the return of night to the Arctic. Previously, the constant daylight coming from the surface, even at depth, made it impossible to detect this phenomenon in the natural environment. With the return of darkness, we could collect microalgae, jellyfish and bioluminescent ctenophores. Analyses using scanning electron microscopy revealed two serious candidates among 20 species of microalgae to explain the «shining sea» phenomenon that has been observed (*Tripos horridus* and *T. furca*).

This work in the polar environment, combining expedition, deep diving and on-board science, has made it possible to study remote sites in the Arctic Zone at depths that are difficult to access. We were able to acquire the first information on the natural fluorescence and bioluminescence capabilities of arctic undersea species and to identify candidate species with potential new properties. The knowledge acquired during this first exploratory work will serve as a basis for developing interdisciplinary research into new proteins in targeted species. ∎

The divers spot fluorescent patterns using lamps that emit UV or blue light. Marcel then analyses the images in a makeshift darkroom in a cabin on the boat.

in order to detect these phenomena in the natural environment. Therefore Keldan® LED dive lamps that emit red light were used to distinguish bioluminescence, while lamps emitting UV or blue light made it possible to reveal fluorescent patterns. We fitted the divers' masks and camera lenses with yellow filters to allow the suppression of UV or blues, meaning only the emitted fluorescent light was discernible.

The DC3 landing on the pack ice in 2010 during the Deepsea Under The Pole by Rolex expedition. According to the former manager of Ken Borek Airline, such a landing would not be feasible nowadays because of the deteriorating condition of the ice. In fact, they haven't made a drop-off at the Pole for several years.

RESOLUTE BAY,
7 YEARS ON

8ᵗʰ August

To us, Resolute was at first an intriguing, mythical feature on maps of the Arctic. A spot that marks one of the most northerly villages on the globe, but more especially the historic American base camp for all polar expeditions. Similarly it had been our base camp where we made our final preparations before setting off for the Pole in 2010.

Seven years have gone by and this time we are returning by sea. Dropping anchor, we found it hard to recognize Resolute village. We had first been there in March, in temperatures of around -40 to -45°C, deep in snow and surrounded by pack ice; now we find ourselves looking at a dusty village beside a beach. The summer thaw often robs these villages of their picturesque appearance by melting their white carpets. There are no signs of hitched-up dog sleds, either. Returning here stirs up buried memories and emotions. Very powerful emotions, just as intense as the exceptional, extraordinary times we experienced here, when our minds, bodies and senses combined with the environment to meet the challenge we were facing: preparing for a successful expedition on the pack ice in the heart of the Arctic Ocean. The place has hardly changed and every building, every warehouse, every track reminds us of the time we spent here. But more than merely jogging our memories, Resolute brings home to us just how deeply we were marked by the experience.

In the hall of the "South Camp Inn" hotel we meet Aziz, the manager, who had helped us with logistics and the delivery of supplies by parachute. He offers us hot showers, access to washing machines and wifi – terribly slow but wifi nonetheless! Our hearts go out to Erwan and Adrien of the yacht Kerguelen who are also attempting the Northwest Passage and we invite them to a meal on board the WHY that evening.

On the only road between the village and the airport we relive those moments spent in the polar twilight, mentally going over our daily to-do list, while watching the surrounding arid hills, so typical of these polar regions, pass by. Returning to the large hangar of Kenn Borek is like a pilgrimage. The yellow glow of the indoor light bulbs, the smell of kerosene, the oil marks splattered on the ground, the green colour of its huge metal doors vividly remind us of preparing our pulka sleds and conjure up the sight of our equipment meticulously laid out on the ground on this very spot some seven years ago. Outside, we find our DC3, the same one that carried us to Eureka and then to the Pole at the end of a fantastic flight such as we will probably never experience again. Not just for the magnificent landscapes that passed beneath our eyes but above all for the heightened emotions we were feeling at the time. The memories had faded but everything here at Resolute brings them flooding back to us.

Seven years earlier we flew in this aircraft towards the geographic North Pole. The flight – and the almost acrobatic landing – were the most epic of our lives. A journey without a passport or a bank card, in one of the most inhospitable places on the planet.

In a gale, the team steer while talking by radio to the crew of the yacht Kerguelen, which they took in tow after they had lost their mooring.

PEEL SOUND,
MAKE OR BREAK

10ᵗʰ August

We set sail at midnight on the 10th of August for the iciest stage of the Passage. Over the years we have learnt that all the lights are seldom at green; often you have to trust your intuition and set off on amber. By intuition, I mean a clever mix of daring, experience and luck! We sail without incident until the next evening, when we are caught by a gale. We are thinking about anchoring when the Kerguelen contacts us; they had lost their anchor just before we reached the area. We decide to tow them behind us. The sea bed here is in poor condition so we start the engine to make our way to a better anchorage. We set off again in the early hours, taking turns on watch while zig-zagging through the sea-ice, sometimes stopping still or turning back when the fog comes down and nothing is visible, even from the crow's nest. Over the VHF radio we chat and sing songs with the Kerguelen's crew to cheer them up. The pack ice grows thicker and starts closing around us. A new ice chart indicates that it will become much too thick for us to carry on. We hope the wind that is forecast will push away the sea ice. While waiting, we moor to the ice and drift at its pace. On board the WHY, the sounds of ice grinding and cracking against its hull create a palpable tension in everyone.

We may be prepared for this situation but we still feel vulnerable. Without mentioning it, we imagine having to overwinter here. Immobilized, helpless, we suddenly spot the lord of this land a few yards away. A huge male appears first, then a mother and her two cubs who must be in their second year. They instantly distract us from our worries. Despite their imposing build, the adults move with agility whereas the youngsters are still clumsy; they seem to be in good health, no doubt because the amount of ice in this region offers them a vast hunting ground.

I love these moments, I love these places. I won't say "above all", but I love them especially because their extreme rarity lends them a purity and richness. Here in Peel Sound we are at the heart of the wilderness in all its splendour. All around, wherever we look, there is no sign of civilisation, nor has there been for days: no hunter's cabin, no stake, no cairn, not a plane in the sky, no rusty diesel can abandoned on the shore by an expedition or a team of Inuit hunters. Here we can see, hear and feel that we are far from everything. Above all, the picture is relatively simple: onshore, the surrounding hills are nothing but an arid desert of yellow pebbles; around us, the sea seems to have disappeared, overwhelmed

The WHY makes difficult progress until it is blocked in the pack ice.
We can no longer manoeuvre in these conditions. We tie up to a floe
to drift at the same speed as the ice while waiting for the wind to pick
up and disperse it, opening up a channel.

The polar bear (*Ursus maritimus*) is, together with the Kodiak bear, one of the largest land carnivores. It is perfectly adapted to its habitat: a white coat for camouflage but black skin to absorb heat, with large, slightly webbed paws that avoid it sinking into the snow and allow it to swim a dozen miles or more. A mother and her two cubs, about 2 years old, are nimbly climbing the cliffs. They are looking for the eggs in the numerous nests sheltered in the crevices of the rocks. The weaker ice pack in summer makes seal hunting more difficult and the bears must be opportunistic.

by thick, compact sea ice, which is constantly whispering to us how small and insignificant we are. And then the sky, burdening everything with its grey weight, lends the landscape a solemn and austere aspect, as if to remind us that yes, life here is hard and precious. In this simplicity and apparent desolation, every moment, every thing has its place. Here, the concept of value is not a theory, it is felt: the world's own order returns. More than the landscapes, it is this lesson, a benevolent reminder of Nature, which endows these places at the end of the world with all their richness.

This time spent in Peel Sound shatters our society's consumerist model, which tries to make us believe that happiness is measured by the acquisition of goods, to the detriment of what is essential: the expression of our senses. Man has lost his way in our world, he is straying, no longer knowing where or who he is. In refocusing life onto its essence, the Arctic reminds us that reason, wisdom and of course happiness are probably better sought for on the road to restraint. Every one of us would benefit from rethinking the real value of things, by remembering what it is that gives memories their power, by seeking out the emotions aroused by profound interactions and by refocusing our lives around a better balance between people and nature.

A team goes to dive beneath the ice and at last we succeed in finding an anchorage that will shelter us from the drifting ice and strong winds to come. We occupy our time by making some scientific dives while awaiting our liberation. When the gales clear away the ice floes blocking the strait, opening the way to Gjøa Haven, we set off downwind under full sail with smiles on everyone's faces.

While we are blocked in the ice, the divers take advantage of the opportunity to dive under the thick pack ice of Peel Sound. Beneath their flippers is a deep blue, above them a ceiling of ice sculpted by the summer melt.

Dives in polar conditions, even when they are short, are testing and hard-won. The cold, the current, the concentration required to swim safely, the preparation time and the time needed to warm up, all make the dives tiring and painful. These difficult conditions, combined with the exceptional landscapes they can offer, make them intense and rare experiences.

GJØA HAVEN,
LOUIE KAMOOKAK,
LIVING MEMORY

On display in Gjoa Haven is the bronze statue of Roald Amundsen, the first explorer to cross the Northwest Passage in 1906 and who subsequently reached the South Pole.

17th August

The sea is glassy and the night inky black when we anchor in the little village of Gjøa Haven, named after Roald Amundsen's ship that overwintered there for almost two years (October 1903–August 1905) before conquering the Northwest Passage for the first time. He found there not only shelter but above all the generous help of the local Inuit – the Netsilik – who taught the Norwegian explorer and his crew how to dress appropriately and survive the Arctic by hunting and fishing. The wisdom that Amundsen gained from their local knowledge allowed him to succeed where so many had failed or perished, especially during the conquest of the South Pole, which he reached with disconcerting ease in 1911 while the English explorer Scott and his men perished there.

At Gjøa we rediscover some of the charm and colour of Greenland's villages, unlike many other communities in the Canadian Arctic that have often been overrun by prefabricated buildings. We dive beside the village to take samples before meeting up again with Louie Kamookak, a historian known around the world for having helped to track down the Franklin expedition's shipwrecks. Louie and his wife welcome us to their home, despite his having returned from hospital by plane that same day[1]. Like most Inuktituts and Greenlanders he is proud, generous and very straightforward. During the evening he opens his archives for us and explains that his passion for Franklin began with a story told to him by his great-grandmother when he was still a child. She described finding artefacts around the island when she herself was only six or seven years old. Forks and spoons that they didn't know how to use, parts of a musket... and a little further off, a great chain leading towards the ocean. Little Louie's curiosity was aroused, to be rekindled at school some years later when a teacher told of Franklin's men, who had died close to King William Island. This clicked with Louie, who made the connection with his great-grandmother's story. Over more than 30 years he recorded memories from the older generation, linking them to the explorers' accounts and reconstructing part of history. His work would play a key rôle in finding HMS Erebus and HMS Terror. It was a lesson in humility for the Europeans and Canadians who had spent decades and put immense effort into their research without ever thinking of consulting the Inuit. Louie is a cultural link, proud of his heritage and tirelessly involved with young people in his community to pass on the oral traditions between generations.

---

1   Louie Kamookak had serious cardiac problems. He died from his illness less than a year later.

Louie Kamookak welcomes us to his home. His great kindness, his commitment to the preservation of Inuit culture, and the story of his life devoted in large part to the reconstruction of Franklin's story, make this meeting a highlight of the Passage. His contribution to finding the wrecks of HMS Terror and HMS Erebus emphazises the importance of oral tradition and has earned him honours and decorations from the Canadian government.

Opposite: Children in Gjoa Haven. Food, soft drinks, television series... The new generation seems more than ever to be under the influence of North America. This loss of cultural references worries the older generation, such as Louie Kamookak, who visits schools to explain the importance of traditional culture.

Above, top: Quad bikes and scooters have replaced sled dogs in most of the villages we passed through.

Above: In Gjoa Haven village, "grizzlar" skins are drying in the open air: the name is a combination of grizzly and polar. These animals are a natural cross between polar bears and grizzlies. In the past, the two species had separate territories, far apart, but due to climate change, grizzly bears are hunting further and further north. These hybrid animals, with coats that vary between white and brown, are known to be powerful and aggressive.

The story of Julia Ogina's great-grandmother is tattooed on her forearm.

On land and ice,
Polar bears, her father and her husband,
Trapped beneath the sky.
All their journeys
On land and ice,
And all the animals trapped,
Beneath the sky.

CAMBRIDGE BAY,
A HERITAGE OF TATTOOS

21ˢᵗ August

At Cambridge Bay we meet Julia Ogna and her companion Jerry Puglick, who have only just landed. Like Louie, both of them fight to keep Inuktitut culture from being forgotten. At sunset, they take us to the other side of the port to see how the climate is changing and witness its effects on the wildlife, such as the arrival of grizzly bears in polar bear territory. Julia, who has recently had her face and forearms tattooed, tells me what the designs represent: the story of her birth, and of her ancestors and their relationship with nature. Tattooing, a tradition among women in the Inuit culture, disappeared almost completely with colonialism and the arrival of missionaries. Spurred on by a woman, Hovak Johnson, who trained in different traditional tattooing techniques, many women are now reconnecting with the tradition. The trigger for Hovak was the disappearance of the last tattooed Inuk woman in Nunavut. She tells of having felt "like a kick in the stomach on realising that another part of their culture could disappear forever".

Julia encourages other women to get tattooed, considering it "as an aid to understanding their history and finding their symbols." She worries that their Inuinnaqtun language (spoken in Cambridge Bay, Kugluktuk and Ulukhaktok) could disappear from here within two generations. "If our language goes we might as well say that our culture has gone", she explains.

Leaving Cambridge Bay, Julia's final words stay in my mind: "even if numbers of us don't speak our language, it is still inside us. Their ears, their eyes, their emotions have been exposed to Inuinnaqtun. There is hope for our language." The ice and the bears aren't the only things to need protection in the Arctic.

Julia Ogina proudly displays her facial tattoos. She encourages young people to reconnect with their culture, which includes tattoos and elements of oral tradition such as language, dance, song, music, stories and legends.

BERNARD HARBOUR,
A WRECK IN THE STORM

24ᵗʰ August

A gale forces us to shelter in Bernard Harbour. The maritime map shows a wreck a few hundred yards away from us. Flying over the area, the drone confirms this discovery: beautifully preserved, it will be the site of our research throughout several dives. As is so often the case, this wreck is an island of biodiversity. Between its imposing ribs, within the hold – preserved by a reinforced structure that has protected it from the ice and storms over the years – we busy ourselves in sampling as many species as possible. The water is clear, the fauna attached to the wreck are superb and a bearded seal pays us a visit. This unexpected stopover will always have a special aura for us, thanks to this mysterious wreck. It is a "Terror" and "Erebus" of our very own.

According to our information, the wreck in Bernard Harbour
was a supply ship for the bases of the DEW line, the North
American protection line against the former USSR that runs
across the whole region.

EXPEDITION MEDICINE & RESCUE ORGANIZATION

DR VÉRONIQUE MÉROUR AND DR EMMANUEL GOUIN
Expedition and dive doctors

So-called "extreme" environments have always had a magnetic fascination for explorers who, over the centuries, have sought to go "beyond": beyond the ends of the Earth, the ice, the depths... even if it should mean pushing forwards beyond the physical and mental limits of "Homo exploratus". However, as soon as we aim for these "beyonds", the need to include a medic among the members of the team becomes rather obvious.

The job of an expedition doctor begins long before departure. The preparation of the mission is the keystone that will safeguard the following months. Their main objective is to ensure good health, to allow the project to go ahead without jeopardising its enthusiasm or ambition.

A medical evacuation could take several hours or days, or it might even be impossible. It is necessary, therefore, to demonstrate foresight and organisation and, once on the spot, to have a good understanding of the terrain and to be adaptable.

How the medical, physical or drug supplies are to be provided and allocated must, therefore, be carefully planned in advance. For most of the time, these are the only resources available during the expedition, and issues of size, weight, cost, storage and preservation must all be taken into account. The medical provision is optimized to cover the majority of common pathologies and the most serious ones, as well as others that are more specifically related to the environment or the activities that will be carried out. The medic is the guarantor, together with the expedition leader, of the mission's safety; they must be able to respond to the majority of possible medical situations, very often without any possibility of obtaining rapid external assistance. Since a wide range of problems can arise, this activity is, therefore, the point where many medical disciplines meet. It is a constant search to find the right balance between respect for standards of care and the vagaries of the environment, available resources and remoteness. For this reason, many qualities must be combined:

- the *preparation* of a medical provision adapted to the project and the target audience
- the control of pre-existing pathologies, in particular via the rigorous organisation of *advance medical visits* prior to departure
- an exhaustive knowledge of the medical resources of the area to be explored, and the development of *evacuation plans*
- *prevention*, which is a major element: "it is better to prevent situations beyond one's control than to encounter them"
- an *in-depth knowledge* of the risks associated with the specific undertaking and the environment
- the *management*, necessarily multi-faceted, of medical issues
- a certain level of *teaching skill* for training members of the expedition in first aid.

This last point, of information and training, is essential, especially in a context of extreme isolation: the expedition members, fully engaged in their adventure, are thereby made aware of the limits and risks that it entails. Acting responsibly, without alarming people, it is about making them realise that the team's first protector is the team itself.

The remoteness and extreme nature of the dives to be carried out for the scientific programmes during the Under The Pole expeditions led to the decision to take doctors with great experience in emergency and diving medicine.

The expedition through the Northwest Passage was one of those challenges involving long-term isolation, as well as taking place in an environment prone to cold-related pathologies. This voyage was punctuated by extreme dives in the most remote areas between Greenland and Alaska. Despite climate change, this remains a hazardous route today, being at the edge of the icecap spreading down from the North Pole, which can close in on a vessel and condemn it to a forced wintering. In such an environment, explorers and their equipment are put to the test: meticulous physical, logistical and material preparation are essential to ensuring the success of such an adventure.

With DeepHope, the waters of the Pacific distanced us from polar considerations but brought others: heat, infectious diseases, underwater fauna etc. The medical scenario became more akin to normal on-board medicine, with cruises of a few days within the Polynesian archipelagos. Some islands have a medical centre or an infirmary offering a first diagnostic or therapeutic remedy, and if necessary the Joint Rescue Coordination Centre or the Urgent Medical Aid Service (SAMU) of maritime coordination can arrange for medical evacuations by air or sea. In the particular case of decompression sickness, depending on the evacuation times, the doctor could decide on a preliminary therapeutic re-immersion. Although this treatment is not a substitute for evacuation to a hyperbaric chamber, it has, in the past, demonstrated its value when the

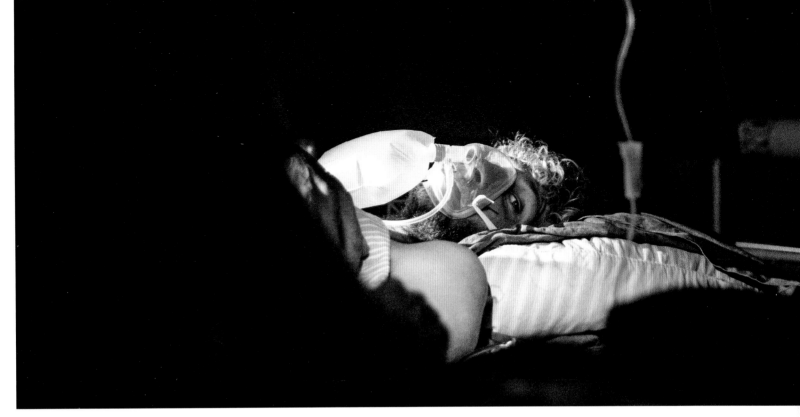

After a deep dive, Nicolas undergoes oxygen therapy for severe fatigue,
probably due to minor decompression sickness.

response time for outside emergency services is too long.

The specific requirements of the Capsule programme centred on saturation diving. On the surface, transfer to Tahiti by helicopter is possible in a few minutes but from the Capsule, the surface was only accessible after several hours of essential decompression stops. Failure to comply with them would inevitably have caused the diver's condition to deteriorate. It therefore seemed necessary to be able to carry out "underwater first aid". Therefore everything was done to enable the diving doctor to go to the Capsule with the appropriate medical equipment to carry out treatment *in situ*, and to allow hyperbaric oxygen therapy to be started.

Whether practiced in the isolation of the polar regions or in the depths of the Pacific, expedition medicine is a subject as vast as the scope of exploration, the barriers of which are being pushed back by technological advances. While the spirit of adventure knows few limits, the context of isolation obliges the expedition medic to prepare for any situation, including the worst, in order to provide the most appropriate response. The doctor or nurse, like any member of an expedition to an isolated location, must therefore be a versatile person: logistician, trainer, preventative medicine worker, general practitioner and emergency physician, field expert... A kind of care "chameleon", whose foresight and adaptability – and undoubtedly a certain dash of daring (which should not, however, be allowed to obscure a measure of humility) – are perhaps some of the keys that will allow the doors dreamt of by many explorers to be opened. ■

Doctors who took part in
the Under The Pole III expedition:

- Greenland and the Northwest Passage:
VÉRONIQUE MÉROUR

- DeepHope: ISABELLE JUBERT, PIERRE
HERRMANN, EMMANUEL GOUIN

- Capsule: EMMANUEL GOUIN, JEAN-ÉRIC
BLATTEAU

1   Shaw MTM, Dallimore J. The medical preparation of expeditions: the role of the medical officer. *Travel Medicine and Infectious Disease.* Nov 2005 ; 3(4):213-23.
2   Iserson KV. Medical Planning for Extended Remote Expeditions. *Wilderness Environ Med.* Dec 2013 ; 24(4):366-77.
3   Lyon RM, Wiggins CM. Expedition Medicine—the Risk of Illness and Injury. *Wilderness Environ Med.* Dec 2010 ; 21(4):318-24.
4   Guly HR. The role of the expedition doctor: lessons from 100 years ago. *Wilderness Environ Med.* June 2012 ; 23(2):170-4.

On the way to Bering we meet walrus
and bowhead whales in the open sea.

TOWARDS THE BERING STRAIT, GATEWAY TO THE PACIFIC

29ᵗʰ August

We stay at Tuktoyaktuk for 24 hours, enough time to have a shower, do some laundry and finish provisioning in preparation for the long voyage that will take us to Nome. Summer is ending and we must head towards Bering before the great autumn storms begin. It is a long, boring crossing, interspersed with regular observations of radar stations on the "DEW Line"[1], solitary islets, sandbanks and above all, the monotony of flat, desert-like landscapes.

Point Barrow features as a turning-point in our long North American journey, between a hidden continent and an ocean of ice that we hope not to see. Point Barrow, like Resolute, Eureka, Prudhoe Bay, Thule or Nome, is intriguing because of its mere presence on the majority of maps. Here, we are at the northernmost point of Alaska, at one end of the Bering Strait and crossing the threshold of the Arctic Ocean. To the south lies a continent, to the north a vast ocean. West lies Russia and behind us, to the east, the American High Arctic. Point Barrow is a crossroads, the furthest west in the world! This inspiring place feeds our imagination. We contemplate it while imagining all the ships that have passed this peninsula in their quests: for the North Pole, for a navigable route to the North Atlantic, or in pursuit of the right whales that come to feed in these waters in summer. Here, summer is short; the nights are already too long to be sailing in a region where ice is never far away. We narrowly escaped it when we were stranded. The sandbanks all along the coast are constantly moving and are poorly mapped as a result. From now on we are heading south, at last! This region may seem like a desert but it is not actually one. Along the way we meet many birds, whales and walruses. The aurora borealis illuminates our night watches. One

1   The DEW Line, or Distant Early Warning Line, was a radar network built by the US across Alaska, Canada, Greenland and Iceland to detect any attempt at Soviet intrusion during the Cold War. It was shut down in the late 1980s.

No more ice but a strong wind and rough sea in the Bering Strait. Emmanuelle returns to the stern, still hanging on after reefing the mainsail to reduce the area of sail.

LIFE ON BOARD IN THE ARCTIC

1. The boat's saloon is alternately a playroom, a dining room, an editing studio, a science lab... 2. Victor cuts Erwan's hair at sea while we are becalmed. 3. Robin helps us at the helm. 4. Tom looking for a toy. 5. Banana communication between Victor, Erwan and Robin. 6. Robin and Tom, "where will we go next?" 7. Twelve people in the saloon for a meal is a tight squeeze, but friendly. 8. Spanish lessons for Tom with Marta. 9. Burger night with Victor and Kevin. 10. Sylvain in the machine room. 11. How to dry clothes in a small space?

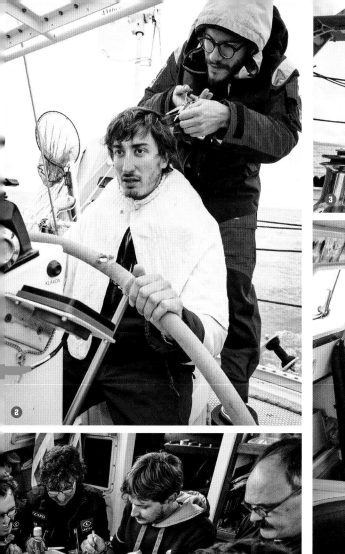

As night returns, the northern lights appear. An amazing sight, they attract the whole crew on deck in a few seconds!

evening, Tom wakes up and we carry him, wrapped in an eiderdown, to see the sky adorned with green. He points his finger at the shining celestial vault, goggle-eyed at the spectacular sight. There is something heavy and hard in this land. Nothing can be taken for granted here; it is always the calm before the storm. On passing Point Hope (ah, these local names!), the wind strengthens, raising a choppy sea. Off Shishmaref the waves surge so high that we can't even see land. The sea is rapidly becoming shallower and the waves build up impressively. We had arranged to meet Vincent, the documentary maker, here, but it is impossible to approach land under these conditions, so we call him on the Iridium[2] to warn him that we won't be able to pick him up as planned and will continue straight to Bering and Nome. Passing through the Bering Strait, the sea is still rough but "cleaner" as we turn the WHY downwind and set off in unforgettable surf, accompanied by petrels hovering over the bow. Looking out at the legendary cliffs on our port side, relief mingles with happiness and pride at having successfully got through the Passage.

2   Satellite telephone.

In the rich waters south of the Bering Strait it is not unusual
to see thousands of seabirds "hunting" at the surface, revealing
the presence of large schools of fish.

Group photo in Nome, the official exit from the Northwest Passage.

In the city of the gold diggers, the bars are still called saloons!

NOME,
AMONG THE GOLD PROSPECTORS

8ᵗʰ September

Nome officially marks the end of the Northwest Passage. Bringing the WHY in to the quay, we are happy with the progress we have made since Uummannaq. But there is still a long way to go before we can shelter from the storms that are starting to descend upon Alaska. Nome is the haunt of gold prospectors who come there to seek fortune and adventure. At nightfall, shaggy haired and tattooed, they fill Nome's pubs. Inside, the atmosphere is like a real spaghetti western saloon. Gildas goes out for 48 hours with some prospectors and comes back with a nugget of the precious metal... which will be mounted, some time later, as an engagement ring! Gaël and Franck go rod fishing for the salmon that pile up in the river. Tom takes his first steps, thanks to being back on solid ground at last. We meet Erik, Krystina and Frances, the skippers of two incredible sailing boats – Snow Dragon and Bagueera – who are returning from an attempt to reach the Pole by sea. Although they did not achieve their goal – which has allowed this happy meeting – they are bringing back alarming statistics about plastic pollution in these latitudes. Our mutual passions – the polar regions, sailing and scientific curiosity – bring us together and convince us to overwinter in front of their house at Sitka.

On the 16ᵗʰ of September we aim for the islands we know as the "stormy Aleutians". For good reason, because we arrive there four days later, after several hours in a storm with hurricane force winds that exceed 70 knots. While Tom sleeps peacefully in his bed, Robin joins us at the map table and curls up with Franck to read his book about aircraft. It's hard to know who is comforting whom. We drop anchor in the pitch-black night at Lost Harbor, hoping that it will hold; admittedly the place's evocative name sets the tone. When we wake, the scenery is amazing. We sail towards Sand Point and then Kodiak, constantly juggling the weather forecasts and the currents. A 35-knot wind counts as fine weather here! The winds are strong but fortunately they are in our favour and the night watches, on an ocean illuminated by fluorescent plankton, are magical.

A muskox beside a waterhole. They live very close to the village of Nome but with their impressive strength, it is best to approach them cautiously, as they do not hesitate to charge when upset.

While sailing in the Aleutian Islands we begin to see green landscapes once again. The winds and currents are strong, and the scenery is breathtaking.

The WHY is battered in choppy seas and winds gusting to 74 knots
(85mph). Everyone is struggling to sleep. Ghislain and Emmanuelle
are between the deck and the navigation station when Robin
snuggles into Franck's bed with his book before finally falling asleep.

Bioluminescent plankton, activated by our wake,
lights up the ocean.

KODIAK,
LAND OF THE BIG GRIZZLIES

25ᵗʰ September

As we near the Kodiak coast, the mist rises to reveal mountains carpeted with pine trees – and a spectacle of fin whales and humpback whales that captivates everyone on the bridge. While in the shelter of the "insides"[1] we admire eagles, foxes and mischievous sea otters swimming on their backs while spying on us out of the corner of their eyes. Alaska is just as we had imagined, its promise is fulfilled; it is as abundant and magnetic as in Jack London's stories. We explore its magnificent anchorages, diving by day and night to collect our last samples. In the port we meet Erik, Krystina and Frances in a pub to celebrate the end of this adventure before most of the crew return home to France. Sailing, hikes and dives punctuate this stopover, during which we are always looking out for this region's king: the Kodiak grizzly bear. Robin and Tom are in heaven at being able to set foot on dry land after all the preceding months at sea.

Despite everything, we dread crossing the Gulf of Alaska to Sitka with a reduced crew. The fishermen on the quay are very concerned about our setting off at this time of year when strings of depressions follow each other in quick succession. A small window of better weather emerges and we cast off on October 13ᵗʰ. On board there are just the children and us, Gaël, Erwan, Sylvain and Jérémy. After an easy four-hour sail we arrive at Goddard Bay, in the Sitka region.

1   Sheltered inlets that are protected from the wind and rough seas.

Alaska keeps its promises. We arrive in Kodiak in the early hours
of the morning to be greeted by a dozen whales in front
of a grandiose landscape, where the pine forests merge with
the misty mountain tops.

Next double-page spread: Kodiak Island is mountainous and
covered with forests in the north and east. Its deep, ice-free
bays allow for navigation and offer safe anchorages despite
the often-poor weather conditions.

Johanna, Scott, Jérémy, Sylvain and Kayak on top of a small
mountain. On the way down from the summit, they come
across a Kodiak bear and her cub who quietly pass on their way.

The Kodiak bear is considered to be the largest land carnivore, along with the polar bear. But it also eats crustaceans, as seen here, meticulously lifting every stone in search of seafood. The nearby fox next to him doesn't seem bothered by the large predator. There is food for everyone!

We dive opportunistically, day and night. The water is clear
and has a few surprises in store for us, such as an encounter
with the bioluminescent jellyfish *Aequorea victoria* (see box,
pp44–45).

The divers plunge into the clear waters of a bay that shelters a kelp forest.
After steep underwater cliffs, rocks, ice and sedimentary sea floors,
this presents a completely new underwater landscape at the end of our
Arctic mission. From time to time, a mischievous looking otter approaches,
swimming on its back, but under water they keep their distance.

The WHY is finally at anchor in Sitka, where it will spend the winter, opposite the property of Erik, Kristina and Frances, our friends who we met in Nome. This small cabin houses a volcanic hot spring with a panoramic view of the bay.

SITKA, PREPARING TO WINTER THE WHY

17ᵗʰ October

As we lie recovering in the hot springs, admiring a glorious landscape disturbed only by the breathing of humpback whales, Erik, who had left port 24 hours after us, encounters a serious gale. We have heard several distress calls on the VHF over the past two days and are beginning to get worried when he arrives at last, exhausted but happy, at the pontoon in front of his house. Erik's neighbours have lent us their quay to unload our kit. We are preparing the WHY for wintering, which will be done in the port of Sitka, and enjoying our friends' wonderful home, which has one of the prettiest views we've ever seen. Tom walks and runs, Robin does paintings of the fjord and Sitka's mountains, we take walks among the totem poles in the park and admire humpback whales swimming past us – or even a school of killer whales! Nature here is so powerful that it is almost mystical.

So ends the long voyage that has led us from the Atlantic to the Pacific through the Northwest Passage, that legendary polar seaway north of America. An extraordinary and difficult journey, as is shown by the small number of vessels – from boats to icebreakers – that are recorded as having have achieved the feat since Roald Amundsen's Gjøa in 1906. Indeed the WHY was only the 27ᵗʰ of them.

On board Under The Pole II, in 2014 and 2015, we explored the Arctic, by diving, from south to north. This time we've done it from east to west! And what a difference! Once again, the richness of the landscapes, depths and species we have encountered all remind us how the Arctic's diversity is matched only by its size: that of an ocean!

In a few months' time we will continue our adventure on board the WHY – and, for the first time, it will be to explore in the heat of the Tropics. After 12 years of expeditions in the cold, the prospect delights us!

It's the end of this leg of the expedition. We prepare the
WHY and our diving equipment for winter. Next destination:
French Polynesia. The dry suits will not be used for a while!

DEEPHOPE PROJECT

PROJECT

LOOKING FOR
THE DEEP-WATER CORALS
OF FRENCH POLYNESIA

THE ALASKA–HAWAII–TAHITI CROSSING

The Pacific is peaceful in name only

At the end of February 2018 we return to Sitka, where we had left the WHY four months earlier, securely moored to the pontoon, while the tremendous North Pacific storms battered Alaska. During this time we had been in France, at our base camp in Concarneau, preparing for the rest of the expedition.

The Capsule project, in particular, had been the focus of our energies. We had been mulling it over for a long time and now, in November 2017, the time had come to transform our ideas, sketches, notes and calculations into a simple, lightweight undersea habitat that would allow divers to live beneath the waves for several days at a time! Scott Cameron, an American engineer, joined our technical team for the occasion. The Capsule project was launched and slowly began to take shape on our computer screens!

These transitional months between two missions are always busy, reviewing what has been accomplished and preparing for future programmes. Often exhausted by many months of communal life on board without a break, it is also a time to recharge your batteries so you can set off again in good shape. A Utopian ideal, as there is so much to do again and again! To mount an expedition is to be forever running out of time. Time to find funding, to prepare equipment and men, to organize logistics and write reports. Team meetings, writing, media interviews... all of which has to be reconciled with the children's return to school and re-establishing our social and family balance. Adventures of

this sort are difficult to lead, which is what makes them so rare and therefore so precious. That is why we have held on and kept going, come hell or high water, for 14 years.

We had reached a new milestone with the Northwest Passage. For us, family life and work often merge. Robin and Tom are growing up and both need constant attention. And, as every parent knows, it is impossible to combine this with a full-time job. Twice we have had someone on board to help us but by the end of the Northwest it was obvious that, with Robin needing schooling and Tom still being so small, we should have a proper professional to come with us. This is how Camille came into our lives. Nanny, home help and soon to be Robin's teacher, she looks after the children during the day while we work. Today, as we are writing this book, Camille is still here and about to start her fifth year with us. She has learnt to sail a semi-rigid boat, swum with whales and sharks, passed her stage 1 diving exam and shares the WHY's best playlist with everyone. Above all she has won our children's affection with a clever blend of tenderness and firmness.

At the beginning of April the time has come to set off. In front of us lies the Pacific, with almost 5,000 nautical miles (5,754 miles) to be covered in two three-week stages and a one-month stopover in Hawaii. At journey's end lies Tahiti, where we should arrive around mid-June.

The Gulf of Alaska lives up to its reputation: strings of depressions follow one another, the wind often reaches 40 knots (46mph), sometimes more, and the sea constantly breaks over the deck.

As a result of experience, Kayak is generally resilient but he hates storms and wedges himself into cramped passages or in the bunk with Ghislain.

During the month that we spent with our friends in Sitka we prepared the WHY for this voyage: she has been scrubbed down, her water and electricity systems maintained, her machinery overhauled, her woodwork restored, her electronics upgraded... in short, we have put her through a thorough annual service so we can set sail with her in top condition. We have also had to "tropicalize" her, because after having mainly served in polar regions, where warmth was of prime importance, we will soon need awnings to protect us from the sun, and will have to produce cold for ourselves with fridges and freezers! But to reach the coconut palms we must head west, vying with the low-pressure systems of the North Atlantic that promise us a rock'n'roll crossing. And it will rock! For this first stage of the voyage there are five of us on board: Armand, the sailor of the group, who will jointly skipper the WHY with me; Gaël, who, after his Northwest adventure, is continuing with us as mechanic and diver; Alexis, who is producing the webcast, and my father, who will fulfil a long-held dream by sharing this crossing with his son. And Kayak, who gets seasick when it is too choppy. Of course, he doesn't like that, being a dog, and a polar dog, as well! Fortunately, all these years on expeditions with us have made Kayak philosophical. But tough as he may be, these two voyages that we are making him put up with – to avoid long stays in quarantine on arrival – don't please him much. For twelve days we endure sailing through the path of depressions on a black or grey stormy sea with occasional white wave crests whipped up by the wind. Setting off so early in the year, we had known that it wouldn't be an easy voyage. The WHY spins up and down on spine-bending, mountainous waves. The masts whistle, the sails propel the

45 tonnes (49.6 tons) of aluminium, diesel, steel, fabric and living souls across the immense North Pacific. We hit gale after gale. The WHY is battered, heeling first to leeward then being struck violently on the other side by walls of water crashing down on her hull. All round us there is nothing, this is our oasis of life. Sitting patiently at our feet, Kayak drools but doesn't throw up. When he isn't with us in the cockpit, coping with the great splashes of seawater that regularly transform our ship into a washing machine, he is on my bed, squeezed in between the hull and the anti-roll board. Like all of us, he braces himself to settle down in the hopes of finding some rest. Often to no avail. At the height of the tempest, which lasts for two consecutive days and nights, I can't sleep. The anemometer is stuck between 45 and 55 knots (52–63mph), frequently gusting to 70 (80mph). I expect the WHY, shaken so violently, to lose a mast at any moment. I imagine the titanic forces being inflicted on the rigging or the centre-board. But she takes it all, absorbing the shocks, moving ever onward. Kayak doesn't leave my bed during this testing time. Two days without defecating or eating, with only a quick lap from the bowl of water that I sometimes bring him. A dog's life indeed.

Manue and I hold a daily meeting over the Iridium. She has arrived in Hawaii with Robin, Tom, Camille and my mother and from there she liaises with the office in Brittany. Leaning back against the bulkhead, feet braced, eyes riveted to the navigation station's screens and with the satellite telephone screwed to my ear, I update her with our onboard news. We discuss the progress that our team in Concarneau is making meanwhile: building the Capsule, developing its electronic air filtration system and its telecommunication system, financial worries, organising for our

Our arrival in Honolulu harbour at dusk is such a striking contrast that
it seems almost magical: surfers and pirogues welcoming the WHY
in the channel, illuminated buildings after weeks of oceanic isolation...
Aloha Hawaii!

arrival... Even at sea, managing an expedition is very down to earth!

Mile after mile, day after night, spring advances and the WHY makes headway towards her destination. And after these first twelve difficult days, in just a few hours, the tropics will welcome us! We swap sailing jackets, snow gear and boots for shorts and tee shirts! The water is warm and has gone from grey-green to deep blue.

The dead calm of the last few days lets us tidy up, do an inventory of the stores, catch up with ourselves in the kitchen and watch a few cult films together. We encounter turtles but mostly we see drifting rafts of rubbish, plastics and cans entangled with nets. On two occasions we have to dive to free the propellers from tangles of fishing gear. At the centre of the planet's largest ocean not an hour passes without plastic pollution, one of the greatest scourges of our time, floating past our eyes. And this is only the tip of the iceberg, since the biggest part of the problem – microplastics – is invisible to the naked eye.

Arriving by sea can't be compared with coming in to land after a flight of several hours. The journey, perspective and emotions are all different. Having had time to look forward to the new destination, to see its shores draw near, you don't feel as if you have been parachuted in. The approach to Hawaii is particularly magical: its islands, its surfers, its fishing traditions, Pearl Harbor and Honolulu, Maui and Big Island... For every sailor, setting foot on land after weeks at sea is a longed-for joy – a deliverance, even. For me, arriving at our destination also means being reunited with Emmanuelle, Robin and Tom. How good it is to hold

them tightly in my arms! They are tanned and as blond as wheat, Robin can swim now and Tom talks even better than he did three weeks ago! Hawaii is a stopover between myth and reality: time to prepare our diving equipment and explore the depths, hike on the volcanoes or in the luxuriant forests, find wild anchorages and others swarming with tourists. Over and over again it means technical and other maintenance but above all it is, for the first time... Under The Pole in shorts and sandals!

We leave the port of Honolulu a month later, at night, which is in itself a spectacular experience, where the twinkling fairyland of skyscrapers overlooking the beaches and coconut palms mingles with the emotion of setting off into the open sea. Tom, in Manue's arms, waves his little hand; today is his second birthday. We have decided that the crossing would be much too long for our two young adventurers, so we will meet up with them again on Tahiti. On board, the crew is still the same, apart from my father, who has returned to France with my mother. So there are just four of us – Armand, Gaël, Alexis and me – plus Kayak, our polar hero who will soon have earned the title of hero of the Pacific!

We tack away from Hawaii in a choppy sea that gives our stomachs a rough ride. The islands have a considerable effect on the winds and surrounding currents hereabouts. After three days we finally reach the southeast point of Big Island, marking our farewell to these volcanic lands. We have sailed to the east to avoid the spectacular eruption that has been in the headlines for several weeks: clouds of toxic smoke pour out across the ocean downwind, west of the island and crossing through it certainly wouldn't be advisable. As we round the eastern point of

Big Island at a distance of 2 nautical miles (2.3 miles), Hawaii bids us farewell in the most improbable way, allowing us to watch a volcanic eruption from the safety of the WHY and the sea. We have sailed past an erupting volcano! The coast and its villas have been abandoned, rivers of black lava criss-cross the slopes, thick columns of smoke rise into the sky: the landscape has obviously been deeply affected in just a few days. The sky is red, reflecting the liquid lava bubbling in the crater, above which we can make out splashes of molten lava leaping several tens of metres into the air. Never before have I seen the Earth spit forth its fire and I will always remember it, for the awe-inspiring spectacle it offers and the telluric power it displays. The WHY is now on a bearing of 150°, and in front of us stretches the Pacific and 2,300 nautical miles (2,647 miles) of open sea before the nearest dry land. But before we fix our eyes definitely southward our fishing lines twitch and we reel in our first two catches: skipjack tuna that will feed us for several days! Aloha Hawaii! Our crossing is bounded to the north by the Tropic of Cancer, to the south by the Tropic of Capricorn and down the middle by the Equator, which is where we change hemispheres. We will spend around three weeks upwind on one tack, to port. To translate for those who are unfamiliar with marine jargon: it will be uncomfortable, monotonous and the heat will be overwhelming.

I have time to immerse myself in reading about the history of the Polynesian people's exploration of the Pacific. A slow, organized colonization that began around 3,300 years ago with the settlement of the Tongan islands, situated at the west of the Polynesian triangle defined by New Zealand to the west, Hawaii to the north and Easter Island to the east. Born navigator-explorers who knew the currents and could recognize the position of a distant island from the colour of the sky and the shape of the clouds, they navigated by the stars and by translating the observations of species of birds, fish and seaweed that they made on their way into geographical information. People whose bravest sailors led well-planned reconnaissance journeys before launching large catamarans capable of sailing against the winds and currents for several weeks with families, food and animals on board. People whose oral tradition handed down a thousand years of wisdom based on observation, knowledge and a deep respect for nature. A culture which, for all this, reminds us in many ways of the Inuit people and which immerses us, as we find out about it, in a different kind of exploration, one that contrasts strongly with the sort that was carried out by Europeans.

On the 9th June 2018 the WHY comes within sight of Tahiti, enveloped in cloud. In crossing the Taapuna channel and entering its lagoon we end a long journey and are about to open a new page of Under The Pole. On the quay, Emmanuelle, Robin, Tom and Camille, who preceded us by plane a week ago, are waiting for us. This is it, we have arrived. Under The Pole... under Polynesia!

Kayak has always taken part in the Under The Pole expeditions: North Pole, Greenland, Northwest Passage, Atlantic crossing and then across the Pacific, he shows exceptional adaptability. He is the team's mascot and Robin and Tom's best friend.

KAYAK

The Under The Pole
expeditions' dog

I remember the day we went to get Kayak. We wanted a dog to go with us on the ice floes and warn us of polar bears. I promised to look after him, to take him to the end of the world, on adventures worthy of Jack London. I tried to prepare him as best I could. I have often doubted him and he has always surprised me. When he was barely a year old he followed us to the geographic North Pole on what was to be the most challenging and difficult expedition we have ever done. In the DC3 that was trying to land us on the ice floe, he jumped onto my lap. I hugged him to reassure him, while reassuring myself. The pilot said goodbye to him as he left, thinking he was too young and frail to survive the conditions of that Arctic spring. When the plane took off again, in the bright sunshine of early March, at a latitude of 87° north, I said to him, "Go on, Kayak, go!" to get us on our way and forget the fear and cold that were gripping me. That evening I didn't put him outside, I gave him half my portion of cheese and enjoyed his warmth on my feet while telling him that everything would be fine. During those 45 days on the sea ice we were inseparable. I relied on him as he did on me. On that floating ice he became my companion for life. I watched in awe as he adapted so well to the Arctic conditions. His fur grew thicker, he pulled harder, he sniffed the ice, a true polar dog! When we returned home, we bought this tiny house in the middle of the forest. Our team laughed and said that we had bought a house for Kayak. And there was more than a grain of truth in what they said, because it gave him the space he deserved. He could sleep in the cool or come into the warmth as he wanted, smell the smells and the tracks, in the night or the morning dew. When Robin came along he welcomed him with tenderness, as he later would with Tom because, although they take a lot of our attention, they are part of his pack. We sold this house to buy the WHY, and took him on board! Once again, he showed resilience and braved storms and seasickness to become one heck of a husky sailor. The joy of seeing Kayak pulling Robin's little sled on Greenland's pack ice! The impossibility of keeping him quiet when we came across whales, seals or bears. The joy of doing the craziest hikes with him wearing his pack. Seeing him cross the Northwest Passage the year he turned eight! When, in the spring of 2018, we took him on board to cross the Pacific, in difficult sea conditions and then in the tropical heat, we thought he would earn the right to run around the *motu*[1] in the shade of the coconut trees, surrounded by his favourite pack of humans. We didn't know that when he arrived in Polynesia, he would test positive for leishmaniasis and that we would be forced to repatriate him to France for 18 months away from us. Tom and Robin refused to let their dog go. Every time I looked towards the bow of the WHY, he was not there. The WHY is just not the same without Kayak, although we can do without the hair he leaves everywhere and the chore of picking up his mess. Fortunately, family and friends took care of him while we were away and he hardly gave us a second glance when we were reunited a year and a half later.

Kayak, my friend, my dog, my companion, my heroic adventurer, you are now twelve and a half years old. We have decided you have earned your retirement, a simple, comfortable life, even though you still refuse to sleep indoors. You love hugs more than ever and always sing when you want our attention. And you will always be the mascot of the WHY. ∎

---

1   The Polynesian word for a small island.

ARRIVAL
IN FRENCH
POLYNESIA

Diving instructor Aldo Ferrucci takes charge of training the team before the DeepHope programme begins.

TRAINING FOR DEEP DIVING WITH REBREATHERS

At the beginning of July, the Under The Pole team is at full strength. Waterproof bags, crates of video equipment and rebreathers are loaded onto the deck of the WHY at Marina Taina in western Tahiti. In a few hours we will set sail for Moorea and Opunohu Bay where CRIOBE[1] is situated.

We are about to embark on the DeepHope project, which is a departure from the projects we have carried out so far. We had long been wanting to develop our expeditions; now we have put in place a structure that makes scientific research one of their foundations.

DeepHope is an unprecedented programme of scientific research into the corals of the mesophotic zone[2]. Also, for us, it is an enormous challenge in terms of diving: for the last twelve months the team has made hundreds of deep dives right across the whole of Polynesia, going down to between 60 and 100m (196 to 330ft) daily, sometimes much deeper. The depth of the dives, the number of them that are planned, their frequency and the duration of the program require extra vigilance from us. It is one thing to make a deep dive, it is quite another to do it as part of a team – and on a daily basis, too.

Safety is the main concern. How to make sure that there are no accidents? Everyone knows that diving is risky. In reality, though, the risks are relative and can be considerably reduced by rigorous organization. In our case it means building a team and training them so that each one is a valuable team-member, able to operate safely in their diving zone, to ensure the safety of others, either while diving or from the surface, while contributing to an organization where everyone plays their part and understands what is going on above and below the water.

As the programme begins we have a diverse team. Some are seasoned technical divers, others are less experienced, but each has earned their place and will play a full part on board. And all of them share that spirit of adventure, based on friendship, mutual support, generosity and respect, that we cherish and feel is essential to succeed in the challenge we are facing. Despite their different levels of experience we hope they will all dive with the same attitude, with the shared codes and safety procedures that everyone has mastered, including the sailors keeping a lookout on the surface.

So this is why we start DeepHope with a month of teaching and training to familiarize ourselves with the procedures

1   The Insular Research Centre and Environmental Observatory.

2   A zone of intermediate depth, from between 30 to 200m (98 to 660ft), where some light is present but not enough for photosynthesis; the limits vary from ocean to ocean.

The authorities in Papeete organize a ceremony. The WHY is decorated in the traditional way with woven palm leaves to bring it good luck. Dances, music, Polynesian songs and the presentation by the town's mayor of some mother-of-pearl shell make this event a symbolic moment, marking our arrival in Polynesian waters.

Previous double-page spread: An aerial view allows us to see Moorea's two main bays: on the left is Cook's Bay and, on the right, Opunohu Bay where CRIOBE is located. The two channels allow entry points into the lagoon, which is itself protected by the coral reef.

Group photo in Raiatea after training with Aldo.

Individual equipment preparation takes 30–45 minutes before each dive.

particular to this mission. On the programme are: simulating breakdowns and rescues; training ourselves to react to increasingly complex situations; manoeuvring with heavy equipment pulled by thrusters; and practising critical emergency procedures while tirelessly repeating safety gestures and protocols so that they become automatic.

We have entrusted the team's training to renowned diving instructor Aldo Ferrucci. Over the course of four weeks we have also sailed and repeatedly dived at sites in the Society Islands archipelago: Moorea (in the Windward Islands) and Huahine and Raiatea (in the Leeward islands). Aldo is a legendary rebreather diver. He is also a remarkable teacher, calm, educational, modest and ultra-experienced, who is equally accustomed to filming and taking photos and videos. On first arriving on board he is somewhat surprised by the lack of privacy that is part of daily life on the WHY, but after a few days it is as if he has always been part of the team. For a month we train alongside him, discussing, testing ourselves, each progressing to their own level. Aldo has the ease and facility of people who have nothing more to prove in their discipline. Fundamentally humane, he is, as well as being an excellent technical instructor, a keenly observant psychologist. He knows how to relieve everyone's particular stress, be it over-tiredness or nervous tension, and can gently untie its threads before a knot can form. He selflessly gives out advice, marvels at each dive and retains a tender, poetic rapport with the ocean. As a good Italian should, he cooks pasta like no one else and makes aperitifs that have become legendary. Thanks to him we start DeepHope calmly confident in each other and our diving abilities. We part from Aldo with regret but with two new rendezvous: he is returning to the Marquesas but he will rejoin us later at Moorea for the entire duration of the Capsule project, as diving director.

We knew that once the programme began we would have to stay vigilant and not relax, despite the lack of routine. Because a twelve-month programme is a long time! Keeping an eye on everyone, noticing their worries, seeing when emotions are running high, being wary of overconfidence, attentive to tiredness, weariness, stress, greed... The greatest risk is the trivialization of an activity, deep diving, that will always be dangerous. So we have to be permanently cautious and maintain strict discipline. Every day we must stand back and take an overview, to decide what can or cannot be done, what is reasonable and what might be dangerous. This is the diving director's role, like the conductor of an orchestra, a key position that can be earned with experience. It consists, in the field, of ensuring that the mission's objectives are proportional and realistically achievable, while always guarding against accidents. On board throughout DeepHope, Julien Leblond, whose experience justifies such a responsibility, will kindly accompany me in this mission.

Returning from a dive. The smiles say a lot about
the pleasure of these long rebreather dives, in clear,
warm waters teeming with life.

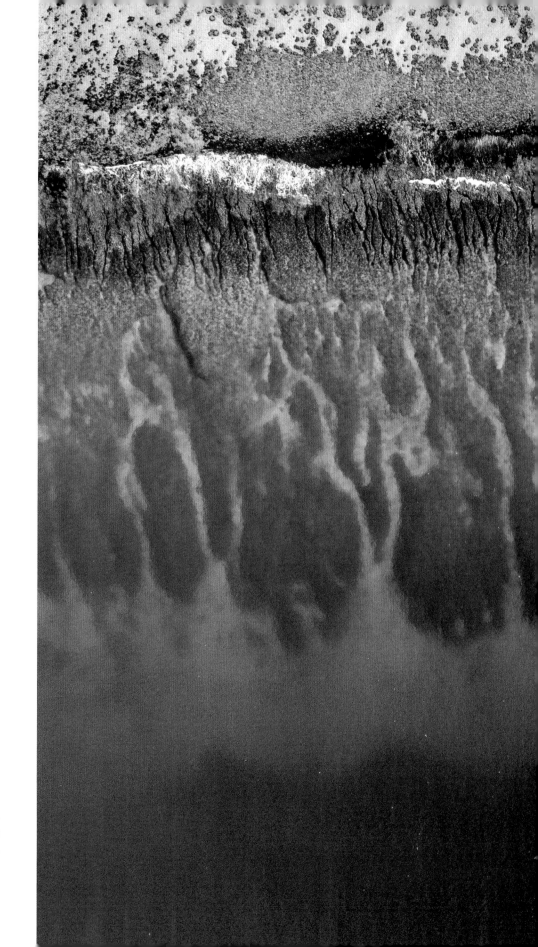

Drone view of the Moorea barrier reef.
On the surface, the semi-rigid inflatable
boat (RIB) ensures the safety of the divers.

Laëtitia Hédouin, DeepHope's scientific director, presents the scientific objectives to the team members.

Learning the distinctive signs of different coral species and genera under the microscope.

THE SOCIETY ARCHIPELAGO

MOOREA

Workshop, the coral school

Opunohu Bay is a microcosm of everything that is beautiful in Polynesia, a turquoise lagoon where turtles, rays and sharks glide, vertiginous mountains edged with tropical forest, a white sand beach dotted with coconut palms and, from July to October, the humpback whales that have come here to give birth. It's not surprising that round-the-world sailors often stay here, having tasted such a paradise. Here, at the start of August, it is time to learn about the science of corals and for the researchers to get to grips with the WHY. To that end, Laëtitia Hédouin, the scientific director of DeepHope, has organized a workshop bringing together scientists and the Under The Pole team so we can learn how to work together. For us, it is like going back to school. But a coral school! Leptoreris, Pachyseris, Echinophyllia, Pocillopora, Porites, Acropora… we discover this special creature's characteristics as well as the many species rated by genus according to the standard classification – and in Latin, if you please! We familiarize ourselves with their structure, how they function, their distribution around the globe. In the rooms and labs of CRIOBE and on board the WHY we alternate presentations, observations with binoculars and taxonomic exercises with Michel Pichon, the doyen of the group, who is a world-renowned expert in the field. We get to know the mission's scientists, who have joined us specially from their research centres around the world. To attempt to answer the questions posed by DeepHope, the data, measurements or samples to be taken while diving are structured into protocols. What species to collect? At what depths? How many samples each time? Which material to prioritize? How to position the sensors and how best to prepare them so that they will be easy to set out during a dive? How many photoquadrat replicas to make, and is the rendering acceptable? We establish a realistic, efficient organisation, thanks to discussions between the coral reef experts and the divers. At last, after two weeks guided by science, the time has come to begin DeepHope. All of us – the divers, scientists, doctor, cook, sailors, technicians, cameraman and photographer – are curious and impatient to come face to face with the mysterious mesophotic corals of the outer slope of Moorea's reef.

Michel Pichon is a world-renowned specialist in the taxonomy (identification and classification) of corals. He started his career with the Cousteau team and soon fires us with his passion for deep-sea corals as well as his curiosity about them.

Reminding us of the Jurassic era, Mount Tohiea
("shark's tooth" in Polynesian) overlooks Opunohu Bay
in Moorea.

First discoveries

Anchored not far from the Moorea channel (our way to the open sea), the WHY is swinging with the wind, its pickaxe-type anchor buried in the silt 15m (50ft) down. A veritable logistics platform for the team and equipment, she is our support ship. She has carried out this role with strength and bravery since we started out together in Greenland in 2014. Heavily laden, she is supported in her work by two rigid inflatable boats. What is usually known as the bridge is here more like a warehouse, stacked with crates, cans of all sorts, diving tanks, the inflation station and other equipment needed for our work.

What shall I say of these Polynesian dives that we do almost daily all along the reef? From a technical point of view they are ultimately very similar to those we have done in the polar zone: apart from a few "details" and a lightweight suit, the equipment configuration and strict diving protocols are exactly the same. We dive with rebreather diving suits fitted with four small bottles (two of oxygen – one of them for emergency use – one for the O_2/He/N_2 mixture[1] that we breathe and one of air to supply the stabilization vest). We each set off with two large emergency bottles, the "bailouts", under our arms. To this we must add flares,

nets for collecting corals, cutting pliers, hammers and chisels for sampling, temperature and light sensors, hydrophones, the photoquadrat for collecting scientific images, and photo or video boxes. To tow it all and to get around quickly and easily, everyone is equipped with a thruster. Compared with the polar dives that we have been used to until now the only real difference is the outfit: into the cupboard goes the thick dry-suit with its bulky gloves, heavy flippers and especially its essential large, heated undersuit[2]. Here, however, a full 5mm outfit coupled with a 3mm neoprene shorty[3] will be sufficient for dives of three to four hours. This outfit is transformative, giving us back our mobility, even though after several deep dives the neoprene feels more like a cigarette paper than a layer of flexible, elastic insulation. No need for slippers or gloves, no more contorting yourself to put on your fins. There's no doubt about it: diving in the Tropics is both simpler and more comfortable than it is among icebergs!

Even more than the temperature of the water, it is its clarity – or the visibility as the divers would say – that gives our dives an unrivalled spatial dimension, putting all other difficulties in the shade. The water is often even clearer at depth than it is at the surface.

---

1   A breathing mixture made up of oxygen, helium and nitrogen.

1   A wetsuit that covers the entire body (trunk, legs, arms and head).
2   A wetsuit that covers the trunk, ending at mid-thigh and mid-arm.

Emmanuelle and Julien sampling on the outer reef. Each sample is put into an individual bag, then in a net and is sent up to the surface by parachute. The scientists on the surface immediately begin their identification and processing.

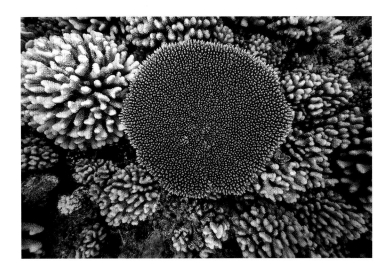

In August 2018, the Moorea reef is healthy, with good diversity and significant coral cover. Unfortunately, it will be severely damaged by bleaching events in 2019 and 2020.

Surveying the reef, which, at around 80m (260ft) down, tilts towards the vertical, our bulky diving suits are forgotten while we try to put our sampling protocols into action. What a theatre!

These first weeks of diving launch the DeepHope programme. Everyone starts to get their head around the job: the divers refine their knowledge and become more efficient, the scientists organize their collections, procedures are tweaked day by day. The scientists are enthusiastic about the first results, which are already reporting new findings while also posing new questions. On board, the diving schedule determines the rhythm of daily life and we are now confident in our ability to roll out our programme throughout the five archipelagos of French Polynesia.

Zero gravity. Diving is surely the closest thing on Earth to what is possible in space.

On each of the 24 sites studied throughout French Polynesia, a minimum of 40 photoquadrats were taken at 120, 90, 60, 40, 20 and 6m depth (394, 295, 196, 130, 66 and 20ft), to map the density, diversity and distribution of species by area and depth.

The characteristic "field of roses" in Moorea is made
up of *Pachyseris speciosa* type corals and is densest
at a depth between 30 and 60m (98–196ft).

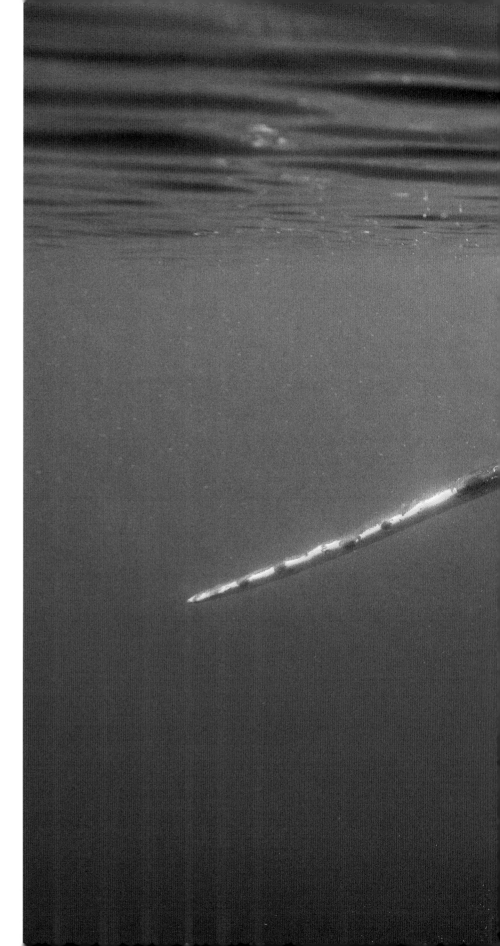

Emmanuelle had promised Robin he would take him swimming with "the big whales". Aged 6, Robin realised this dream and approached several humpback whales and curious whale calves. From July to October, they come to the warm waters of Polynesia to give birth and nurse their young before heading back to Antarctica. Coming eye to eye with a whale is certainly an experience that changes our view of the wild world.

LIFE ON BOARD IN THE TROPICS

1. Rinsing all the diving equipment on deck.
2. Swinging and jumping in the lagoon, the loveliest playground of all. 3. Inflating the tanks.
4. Emmanuelle and Héloïse in the world's most beautiful shower. 5. Stowing supplies. 6. Héloïse and Gonzalo process the data from the CTD, the probe that measures conductivity, temperature and depth. 7. Max edits the webdoc in his "office". 8. Christmas in the Marquesas. 9. Robin and Camille in the kitchen.
10. Héloïse working in good company.
11. Ghislain, champion coconut opener.
12. When the divers have left the WHY, Robin and Camille have a peaceful classroom.

Bora Bora is synonymous with honeymoons and bungalows on stilts,
but this does not do justice to this wild, magnificent island with
its superb sea floor and a lagoon like an incomparable blue mosaic.

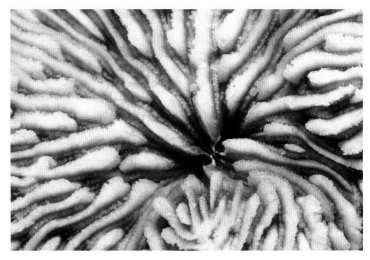

Close-up of coral 805.

BORA BORA

Specimen 805 (by Erwan Marivint)

On the 15th September 2018 we arrive with the WHY at Bora Bora, that legendary atoll in the Society Islands.

Whenever we dive for the first time at a new island location there is an excitement linked to the exploration of the still largely unknown mesophotic zone.

Throughout the dives and conversations with the on-board scientists, our eyes become used to recognising corals, increasing our desire to learn more about them. Our natural curiosity as divers, combined with the scientists' involvement and their wonder at the samples we have collected, only serves to strengthen our motivation.

A "diversity" dive to 60m (196ft) is scheduled that day. The aim is to collect all of the different species of coral present at that depth. At 55m (180ft) the plateau ends, jutting out over a dizzying drop. The blue water is crystal clear as far as the eye can see. Loud whale song and the motion of our thrusters give us the impression of moving in a different world – extraterrestrial perhaps, or rather, abyssal.

Five metres (16ft) deeper we begin sampling in our study area. Beneath our flippers, the lack of light lets us imagine the 300m (984ft) that lie between us and the sea floor.

Little by little we fill the nets, the sign of a successful collecting session. Shortly before returning to the surface, a white discoid skeleton coral fixed to the rock attracts my attention. At the time, I think how interesting it is that the species vary according to the geographical distribution of the archipelagos and the islands, a fact that is explained partly by temperature differences and water turbidity. I am sure that I have never collected this coral before, nor have I seen it among our earlier specimens.

As usual after each dive we share our discoveries with Michel, Héloïse or Gonzalo on the bridge of the WHY, and discuss the underwater conditions and the environment where we have collected our samples. Michel confirms my suspicion that this coral is a novelty, because specimen No. 805 has not been collected before during the expedition. A world-renowned taxonomist, he spends hours with his nose in his books trying to identify it. Although it is a challenge worthy of a specialist it does annoy him somewhat! Some time later we learn the importance of this find, because it is the first time that a specimen of this species and genus has been seen in Polynesia. In later dives we find it again, at depths of between 40 and 90m (130–295ft) in the waters off several islands.

It still has not been confirmed at time of writing whether this species is new to science. Although it is similar to the genus *Cantharellus*, particularly the species *Cantharellus jebbii* found in the Red Sea, No. 805 is still slightly different, proving that the ocean still holds many secrets and mysteries.

Manue and Erwan take samples on the outer slope of the reef. We plan for two types of sampling on these dives: the first aims to collect specific species defined at the beginning of the programme, such as *Pachyseris speciosa* or *Pocillopora verrucosa*; the second is a "diversity" collection, where one of each different species present is collected.

Erwan and Manue travel with thrusters between two working depths. These scooters make it possible to reach the work areas quickly, to stay safe when there is a current and to transport scientific and video equipment without getting tired.

Ghislain and Antoine are working on a steep drop-off at 120m (394ft).
Their next working area will be at 20m (66ft) and then 6m (20ft).
By splitting the depths of their activity, one team's diving times closely
match those of another. This is important from a logistical and safety
point of view.

THE TRIBULATIONS OF A TAXONOMIST

DR MICHEL PICHON
Expert in coral taxonomy,
Museum of Tropical Queensland

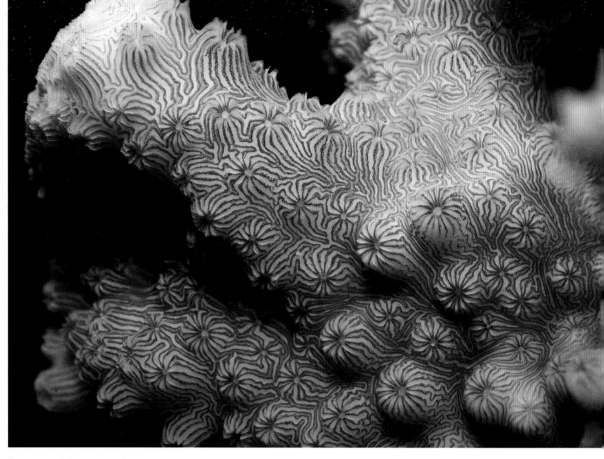

Pavona maldivensis, a scleractinian species, is rather unusual in having a wide geographical distribution. It also has a wide bathymetric distribution, from the surface down to almost 90m (295ft) in depth.

Systematic taxonomy, classification, nomenclature... so many terms, often used interchangeably and, moreover, slightly abusively, that sound somewhat bizarre to the general public. But what, exactly, do they encompass? Simply putting on a diving mask and splashing around over a coral reef with your head dipped into the water is all that it takes to be blown away by the incredible diversity of shapes and colours of this environment, teeming with life. At the forefront of this diversity are, of course, the corals. But how can one make sense of this rather untidy-looking abundance?

That's how it all started for me, because what I found most interesting was who lived where in a reef, and the solution was to impose some order on the chaos. So it would be necessary to group the different types of corals methodically, by category, according to well-defined criteria. Yes, but what criteria to use? Their colour? Not reliable. The general shape of the colonies? That's a little better, but not enough. It is necessary to go into more detail and take into account characters that are often very difficult to see with the naked eye. The advantage of corals is that they have a perennial limestone skeleton (hence the name "stony polyps" that was previously applied to them), a skeleton that is often found fossilized in the strata of terrain that was submerged in previous geological eras. These fossils were much easier to access – until the

recent invention of SCUBA equipment – than the underwater world, even at modest depths. It is therefore to palaeontologists that we owe the method and system of classification of corals, based on their morphology (inward and outward form and structure) at different levels of magnification. This so-called "morphotaxonomic" approach (of which I am a fervent follower, because it is simple, inexpensive, practical to implement and requires few resources) is still very widely used today. It is complemented by different approaches such as molecular genetics, leading to a phylogenetic classification. But it is not enough simply to give order to all this diversity, we must also be able to designate, unambiguously and in a reproducible way, each of those defined

categories: we must name them, in other words define a system of "nomenclature". This system must also be infallible; that is, it must make it possible, in all circumstances, to assign the same name to the same category of organism, the basic category being the species. As a start, imagine choosing a name in everyday language (what is called a "common name" or "vernacular name") based on a very particular characteristic linked to the category in question, for example the colour, or a reference to a known thing or form; as we have already noted, however, this is unreliable. For example, how do you distinguish between cauliflower coral, giant cauliflower coral and lean cauliflower coral? Worse still, these common names vary from language to language and even from region to region. They are still widely used, too often in my opinion, but should be absolutely avoided. What is needed is a universal system that eliminates any ambiguity about what is being designated.

The answer was found over two centuries ago by the Swedish biologist Linnaeus, who introduced the binomial nomenclature system: all living species have a unique scientific name made up of two Latin, or Latinized, words. The first is the name of the genus, a genus being a grouping together of species with strong similarities or affinities. The second word is the name of the species itself. So this unique combination of the two names makes up the species name, which is therefore designated without any possible confusion. Since Linnaeus' day, as a result of the exploration and study of our terrestrial and marine environment, many species have been described. Over time, though, there has been a significant risk of confusion between species, mainly because researchers had limited possibilities of communicating with each other. In fact, to help to guide us and resolve any ambiguity, the very strict rules relating to nomenclature are laid down in an *International Code of Zoological Nomenclature*. Admittedly, being written in legalistic language, it is not an exciting read. But it remains indispensable for the taxonomist, and is a book that I always keep on my desk, close to hand.

To classify and name species, we need collections, which are generally kept in museums, for which this is a fundamental purpose. Unfortunately, for many years, "museum" has suggested somewhere dusty to the general public. Somewhere far removed from the modern world and its aspirations for discovery, where you might possibly encounter some pale, intelligent eccentric, playing with their favourite little animal specimens. An inaccurate perception of the situation, of course, but

one that is strongly encouraged by the scant resources and lack of kudos associated with the far-too-rare official "taxonomy" posts. The result of this lack of recruitment has been the increasing scarcity, not to say virtual disappearance, of taxonomic skills, here there and everywhere.

Should I consider myself an endangered species or a living fossil? Yes, without a doubt! But while taxonomy is often a vocation, it is also a passion, a drug and a constant challenge. And as such, it seems clear that DeepHope has been a permanent challenge: samples of crepuscular coral environments, especially due to the weak light that reaches these depths, take on the most bizarre shapes and structures. They are often very different from what can be seen in shallow reefs, where the samples have been collected that have formed the basis of studies until now.

So, what is it? What name should it be given? – I was doubtful and hesitant before settling on *Psammocora nierstraszi* or *Leptoseris mycetoseroides* (neither name being very poetic or particularly evocative). And had I, after all, used the right criteria to make the identification? One possible answer might be the one that occurred to me that day when, at anchor downwind of the island of Taravai, in the Gambier Islands, I surprised Tom and Robin crunching away with their nice strong teeth at some samples of well-bleached coral that Héloïse had put out onto trays for their daily dose of sunshine! Should a "crispiness" index, both literal and metaphorical, join our array of taxonomic tools? Watch this space! Taxonomy still has a bright future ahead of it...

∎

Once the corals have been collected, catalogued and numbered, they are sampled in tubes for DNA/RNA analysis (a very small piece is enough).
The colonies are then bleached to allow Michel's identification work, sometimes using a microscope.

Above, top: Ghislain positions one of the six sensors that will record light and temperature at the sampling depths over several days.

Above: Thrusters are (along with rebreathers) indispensable tools for DeepHope dives. They allow you to travel long distances quickly, loaded with equipment and without the risk of running out of breath.

Right: Beyond a depth of 70–80m (230–260ft), we sometimes work on vertical drops, where the light becomes in a fainter and fainter until only blue is visible. Corals are, however, still present, having adapted to the more hostile, less suitable conditions.

The incident

"Our relationships with animals and their animal nature are infantilized, primitivized. It is insulting to animals and it is insulting to children. [...] For animals deserve more than infantile or moral consideration: together we cohabit this Earth and share a common ancestry, the enigma of life; it is our responsibility to live decently alongside them."

BAPTISTE MORIZOT, *WAYS TO BE ALIVE*

GHISLAIN BARDOUT: On September 25th we set off for the last dive in Bora Bora, on a magnificent site north of the island. The wildlife is abundant here, with large schools of barracuda, jacks, wrasse, tuna, and a large group of grey reef sharks below 60m (196ft). The layer of mesophotic corals is particularly thick and the scientists note that we are bringing up a good diversity of samples.

We set about positioning the hydrophones and sensors, and carrying out the final sampling. The site is so beautiful that we decide to document it with photos and videos before leaving. Six of us plunge into a heavy sea. Julien and I will cover the depths from 120m to 90m (394–295ft), Manue and Erwan those of 60, 40, 20 and 6m (196, 130, 66 and 20ft). Franck will take photos and Nico will help him. On the surface, Jérémy is responsible for safety, Héloïse and Michel process the samples we retrieve from the bottom, Max takes images on board and with the drone. Aurélie Toninanto, a journalist from the *Geneva Tribune*, is there as an observer. In short, there are lots of people above and below the waves!

JULIEN LEBLOND: On the way down, I savour the pleasure of this last immersion in the waters of the Society Islands archipelago. It promises to be exceptional... The next two weeks will be devoted to getting the boat ready before setting off for the Tuamotu Islands, and so I am aware of the program to come as Ghislain and I recover the equipment that has been continuously recording data at 120m (394ft) for the last few days. We make the most of the opportunity to focus on the complex topography as well as the rich assortment of fish and other organisms that pass before our eyes during our ascent. The visibility is excellent; looking up, I see the silhouettes of our friends who are working at 60m (196ft) as well as those of the grey reef sharks that are patrolling the zone. Right in the line of our ascent, at 80m (260ft), one of them attracts my attention with its unusual swimming action, making slow, calm movements alternately from left to right. Arriving at its level, I can also see that its mouth is half open. Thinking that it is trying to regurgitate a fish, I look to see whether it has been hooked. It shows no obvious sign of aggression but its behaviour intrigues me.

G. B.: After Julien has recovered the sensors from 120m and 90m (394 ft and 295ft) and returned them to the surface by parachute, we slowly ascend using our thrusters. Looking through my camera's monitor I film the underwater cliff face, the scattered corals that become more frequent the higher we ascend, the schools of fish scattering in front of me and, in the distance, seeming tiny on

my screen, Julien who seems to have stopped. Getting to within 20m (66ft) of him I can make out what has held his attention: a grey reef shark that is behaving oddly. Twisting from left to right, it swims very slowly in a most unusual manner closer to the corals. Julien watches it for a few moments, then half turns and moves away 30m (100ft) or so. Motionless, I continue filming. The shark passes in front of me and continues on its way. Then it returns the other way and heads along the reef towards Julien. Now moving away from me, it is getting closer to him but has stopped swaying from left to right.

J. L.: A short distance away, I notice a notch in the reef and decide to take a closer look. Ghislain keeps the shark in his camera monitor as I move away. Having satisfied my curiosity I turn back again and distinctly see it leave the wall and swim towards me in the blue. Pulled by my scooter, we meet and for a few seconds it escorts me through this incredible scenery.

The black of the abyss allows me to imagine the dizzying depths beneath my flippers. By contrast, when I raise my eyes they are bathed in an almost blinding light that brings the surface clearly into focus. I am about to leave the shark by veering round to find Ghislain when things take a wholly different turn. Time seems to stand still, or at least to slow down appreciably… I see the shark make a perfect about-turn with a great flick of its tail fin, it opens its mouth and I close my eyes as its jaws close onto me. I am in blackness, helpless, surprised, but its teeth on my skull leave me

in no doubt as to what is happening. I feel no pain, I just register that everything has changed and I am now in a more than precarious situation…

G. B.: It is such a spectacular sight. Julien and the shark are moving side by side in the magnificent blue depths when, in a fraction of a second, the shark turns 180º and rushes towards him. Dumbfounded, I see my partner swaying in a cloud of bubbles, knocked backwards by the impact. I start up my scooter to join him, yelling "Julien" several times into my mouthpiece to let him know I'm coming. After what seems to me like an eternity – but which is really only three seconds – the shark lets go and rushes excitedly towards me. Everything moves very quickly, I am wary of its intentions but it turns at right angles in front of my camera and goes back to the reef behind me. I then head towards Julien as quickly as I can.

J. L.: With water in the closed circuit of my rebreather and my mask torn off, I automatically grab the regulator of my spare bottle as I hear Ghislain shout. The distinctive sound of his scooter starting confirms that he has seen it all and that he is already heading towards me. Stay calm, follow the protocol and remain confident. At this point I am dealing with the situation and my feelings on my own; if I let myself panic it could be fatal. I breathe as calmly as possible, knowing that I have plenty of gas to ascend to 20m (66ft) without difficulty.

G. B.: Arriving by his side, ready to give him my back-up regulator, I see his mask leaking, its strap cut. I move level with him so that he can sense that I am there. I make a large OK sign in front of his face so that he knows that I am there and the shark has gone. Without his mask, Julien's sight is blurred. His eyes are wide open, huge, hallucinating. Bubbles stream from his rebreather's circuit in several places, his hood is damaged, but he seems to be in control of the situation and switches to his safety mask by himself. We are still 80m (260ft) down and time is ticking by, we must return to the surface as soon as possible. Nico joins us and I hand him my yellow parachute[1] to confirm that the situation is as serious as the look in our eyes is telling him.

J. L.: I get my back-up mask and change the settings of my decompression instruments because I am now using an open circuit system. Then I signal Ghislain that "all is well" – or as well as can be expected. We quickly reach the reef for our first minutes of mandatory decompression stages, around 60m (200ft). The other group, somewhat shocked, find us and send an alert up to the surface. Nico triggers the yellow parachute and then gives me a look that says much more than any hand signal ever could.

G. B.: Back together, we form a unit, as if to reassure ourselves. Now, at 55m (180ft) we are in the rhythm of decompression stages, which we have to take every 3m (10ft). I explain to everyone what has just happened and make a quick mental assessment of the situation: Julien's rebreather is out of action, his wounds are not visible but he seems to be losing a lot of blood and we have two and a half hours of mandatory decompression before we can surface. It is an awkward situation but happily Julien seems calm and in possession of his faculties.

J. L.: Ghislain is keen to find out the extent of the damage and although he seems to have mixed feelings he is not distraught when I remove my hood. Beside me I just see a huge green cloud[2] dispersing above my head. The boat's engine roars and less than five minutes later we see the emergency decompression line descending (which will allow me to complete the stages) and also the white writing slate that lets us contact the surface. I have almost two and a half hours before I can get my head out of the water. I try to go back onto the rebreather but the shark's teeth had got the better of the mouthpiece's corrugated pipes and the machine is flooded, unusable. I focus on the fact that everything will be all right, we are now above 50m (165ft) and the sharks are no longer with us. They have

1   A yellow parachute is sent to the surface to initiate the safety procedure. Red parachutes are used for lifting samples, other material or for sending signals to the surface.

2   Colours disappear progressively with depth, leaving nothing but blue. Thus at a depth of several tens of metres (tens of yards), red, and therefore blood, appear as very dark green.

stayed down in the deep zone, just as we have seen them do on previous dives. Only one thing is uncertain: can I remain conscious for all the time required for decompression? I feel relatively well and confident but I don't know how much blood I'm losing. The next two hours promise to be long but I have a good team around me. I'm not suffering and the safety diver has come down to assess the situation and report back to the surface team. The doctors on board the WHY must already be preparing the necessary equipment for my care.

G. B.: The safety protocol is in force, we must resurface slowly, one stage at a time. We keep an eye on Julien's condition. Decompression is always time-consuming on these deep dives, but right now it seems particularly so. We all think about what has just happened, playing it over in our minds in an attempt to understand. The haemorrhaging seems to have stopped, which is reassuring. His gaze is scarred by abnormal fatigue. Every time I question him, he invariably replies that "It's OK".

J. L.: I go over the events in a continuous loop in my mind but I can't work out what could have triggered such behaviour. I am not a shark expert but I have often dived among them and I know the intimidating swimming style that they can adopt if they feel annoyed or excited. When I had been able to observe it, it was much more typical: jerky, more nervous and quicker than this time. It is accompanied by warning signs such as closer passes or even clearly aimed charges, but never has anyone described to me such a sudden change in behaviour without a particular stimulus... Once I have ascended to 15m (49ft) I'm sure that the dive will be a success, I have all the gas I need to complete the stops and I still feel in good shape. I'm just looking forward to phoning my wife to hear her voice and tell her about this mishap, while hoping that I don't end up shaven-headed!

G. B.: At the end of the afternoon we emerge at last. We rehydrate ourselves, eat cakes and bananas, and even have a laugh, as if to relieve the tension of the hours spent underwater. Back on board the WHY, Julien gets away with twelve stitches in his head; to his great relief, the two doctors on board have managed to keep his hair, he is only shaven around where he was bitten. With hindsight, in discussion with the experts and reviewing the scene (fully captured on film), we understand with hindsight what motivated the shark. Its slow, jerky swimming motion was one of intimidation, a mark of territoriality. Misled by its slowness, neither Julien nor I could interpret it correctly at the time. Perhaps we encountered an individual that is more maladjusted than others of its kind; annoyed by our forays into its territory in the preceding days it ended up biting suddenly, with no other warning than this strange swimming. Another hypothesis put forward by an expert is that the scooter had triggered the attack.

From a diving point of view, the accident was extremely serious. Its fortunate outcome is mainly thanks to Julien's remarkable composure and his years of diving, as well as the team's training and our well-organized dives. This event brings home to us even more emphatically just how strongly we are committed to this programme. In addition to the purely technical aspect of these deep dives, there is the environmental dimension. Encounters with schools of grey reef sharks may be common in the channels of French Polynesia, but most happen with divers using open circuit breathing systems (their bubbles keeping fish at a distance), at rather shallower depths and often in the same locales. It is likely that the sharks that we met in the deep zone are much less accustomed to encountering divers. At a time when approaching sharks has become ultra-trivialized by the Go-Pro[3] generation and constant image uploads to social media, the incident reminds us that with every dive we enter a wild habitat that should be approached humbly.

The incident has a lasting effect on the entire team: the impossible has become possible. We now observe the body language of the grey reef sharks – and other species – very carefully, and see this intimidating swimming stance on two more occasions, at Tikehaku and in the Marquesas. From now on, however, we immediately take the only valid course of action: move away safely but without being too hasty!

3   A mini-camera widely used in outdoor sports.

GREY REEF SHARKS: STAY OUT OF MY BUBBLE!

DR ERIC CLUA
Marine biologist, shark specialist
Centre for Island Research and Environmental
Observatory (CRIOBE)onmental Observatory

Who would ever have imagined that sharks are territorial animals? Very few people, probably, because as land animals ourselves we think that everything is different in that hostile underwater environment where we cannot breathe. Everyone has learnt and understood since their earliest childhood that a dog shut in a fenced garden will defend its "territory" by barking to deter any intruder from entering its clearly defined space. Who would be so stupid as to jump over the railings and risk being bitten? No-one, probably, for everyone knows that the dog is territorial and aggressive towards anyone who enters its space without warning. The question is: do sharks do the same thing under the sea? The answer: "Yes, although with certain differences." Yes, because sharks, especially certain species such as the grey reef shark, Carcharhinus amblyrhynchos, are very sensitive to the distance between them and any animal (including humans) that might potentially pose a threat to them. The American scientists who worked on the matter in the 1960s defined three zones, by decreasing distance from the intruder: the zone of vigilance/distrust (from 5m [16ft]; the shark shows signs of potential aggression), the escape zone (between 5 and 3m – [16–10ft]; the shark moves away

to lessen the potential risk) and the zone of aggression (generally less than 3m [10ft]; the shark senses danger and can trigger a defensive bite) (Johnson, 1973). The distances indicated are purely indicative, as the researchers noticed that it was not simply the distance but rather the speed that the diver was swimming at that determined the behaviour of the shark, or its sense of feeling cornered without an escape route, if it were accidentally trapped (whether against the sea bed or a rock face). Unlike a dog that barks to warn off intruders, the shark has very little choice in how to frighten away the diver: firstly, it lowers its two pectoral fins by a few degrees (not necessarily easy to spot), then it adopts a jerky swimming motion by increasing the rigidity of its body (easier to recognize); it also twists in all directions in a distinctive kind of frantic dance. These signs and expressions usually precede the bite that is given if we are unfortunate enough not to move away or let the animal escape. That is what happened to a diver of the Under The Pole team in French Polynesia, 80m (260ft) down, when, using a submarine scooter, he followed a stubborn grey reef shark that had adopted this intimidating attitude. Without realising or intending to, the diver had crossed the distance limit and triggered a defensive bite on the head that, without his thick suit and the expert help of two seasoned professional divers, could have had very serious consequences. Just as in "land territory", distances and the attitude of the intruder play a crucial role in triggering the animal's aggression, but there are some notable differences. Firstly, on dry land, the dog's "territory" is a well-defined, fixed zone; the animal only adopts this territorial attitude towards the place that it knows well. This can also be true of those sharks whose preferred habitat is, for example, a well-identified passage through the coral reef. But most of the time we should understand that it is instead

A school of grey reef sharks in the Hao channel.

the shark's "territory" that moves around with it, so we should rather think in terms of a "personal security space". Next, the dog's territory is basically two-dimensional (a flat surface). With the shark, though, we must imagine a three-dimensional space, a personal "bubble", called an "idiosphere" by scientists (Martin, 2009). In other words, there is no need to be on the same horizontal plane as the shark (like the Under The Pole diver) in order to be bitten, you could also approach from above or obliquely with the same result!

Is this dangerous? Obviously any shark bite is dangerous, particularly because of the haemorrhages caused by the scalpel-sharp teeth. But it must be stressed that this bite is not made with the intention of killing the intruder, just as the dog does not aim to bite and kill in defending its territory. The shark

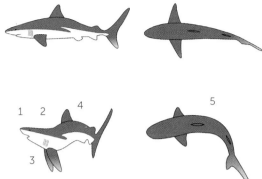

Comparison of normal behaviour (top shark) with aggressive behaviour (bottom shark) in grey reef sharks (after Johnson and Nelson, 1973): 1. snout up; 2. dorsal neck flexion upwards; 3. pectoral tightening; 4. back flexion downwards; and 5) exacerbated lateral body twist.

does not intend to feed itself by eating the diver, and the rather superficial bite does not lead to large losses of flesh and muscle, nor is it life-threatening for the victim (unless a large artery is affected).

Shark bites on humans are globally rare on a planetary scale, around a hundred a year. Fatal bites, barely 5 to 10%, are generally motivated by hunger, when a large shark seeks to feed on humans and then delivers serious bites. The other bites, making up the large majority (more than 90%), are superficial and non-fatal, including defensive bites. Although these last are among the most frequent, they have been happening much less often during the last few decades. They were very frequent in the 1960s, when the undersea depths were opening up to humans thanks to developments in diving, because sharks were coming across

this new "animal" for the first time, this intruder that potentially threatened their safety. In succeeding decades it is probable that, as nautical activities have increased and man has become omnipresent on and below the water, sharks have grown used to the presence of humans and have learned not to react (not to say "over-react") every time they encounter a human (which would be an enormous waste of energy). This analysis holds true for the first 40m (130ft) beneath the surface, the region most commonly reached by the vast majority of divers, apart from a few rare exceptions on the global scale. The advent of new technologies such as diving with alternative diluents instead of nitrogen (such as helium) and closed-circuit diving systems (with recyclers), which the Under The Pole divers specialize in, has opened up new "vertical" depth

horizons to mankind, hitherto very limited by decompression problems. And if some sharks have decided to become used to people, others have, by contrast, decided to live, or stay, in the depths. Is it therefore legitimate to think that the Under The Pole pioneers, like the American divers of the 1960s who paid the price in water 20m (66ft) deep, were attacked at 80m (260ft) down by a shark that had never seen a frogman in its life and simply reacted as its "virgin" grey shark instinct suggested, an instinct that hadn't altered since the 1960s...? ∎

TAHITI

In Polynesia, almost everything starts with Tahiti: you arrive there by plane, you transit there, get supplies, and work. The island brings together two thirds of the entire population of the five archipelagos: the Society Islands, the Tuamotus, the Marquesas, the Gambier Islands and the Austral Islands. For us, too, it was Tahiti where our Polynesian adventure began. But for DeepHope it would be the last island to be studied, the twelfth. Our first dive site, on the northwest side of the reef, would be the White Valley, known the world over for the tiger shark sightings organized there by local clubs practising "scenting" or "chumming"[1]. The second would be further south, also on the west coast, opposite Moorea. For ten days, in the early stages of the Capsule project, we continue diving using rigid inflatable boats operated from the WHY, which remains moored at Taina Marina. For the time being we are studying the physiology[2] of divers who are deep diving using rebreathers. We carry out similar programmes on every expedition, in conjunction with physiological researchers and doctors who are interested in how these dives affect the body, so as to understand them better. Subjected for several hours to high pressures, variable humidity and temperatures, and breathing a mixture of gases other than air, our bodies are tired by these "extreme" dives, which have hardly been studied at all. DeepHope is thus a rare opportunity to study a diverse "population" of divers who are making systematically repeated dives according to a similar profile; the programme makes it possible to extract scientifically valid statistics. In Tahiti, therefore, we sample, measure and collect the usual data from the reef, but additionally, before and after the dives, every one of us undergoes a battery of phsiological tests!

1   The practice of attracting sharks with pieces of fish placed in a cage so that they emit a strong odour but cannot be eaten.
2   See pp. 222-223.

A thruster descent is speedy, to limit the saturation time of the divers and therefore their decompression time on the way back to the surface.

Julien Mai, the mayor of Makatea, tells the history of the island, which is closely linked to phosphate mining, which has pockmarked it as far as the eye can see.

THE TUAMOTU ARCHIPELAGO

MAKATEA, THE UNCLASSIFIABLE ISLAND

The island of Makatea is unlike any of the other atolls forming the Tuamotu Archipelago, of which it is part. Nor does it resemble the mountainous islands of the Society Islands archipelago. No, Makatea is unique. As Julien Maï, the mayor of its only village, explains to us: "*Makatea is not a Polynesian word, it is a word that has been Tahitianized later. Makatea is a scientific word. It simply means «white coral». All the atolls in Polynesia and the Pacific of this kind, scientists call them makatea*". Makatea is in fact an ancient coral atoll raised to the surface by the tectonic action of oceanic plates. This unusual origin has made it particularly rich in phosphates, deposited by the breaking down of fossil residues of marine life over the millennia. After they were discovered at the end of the 19th century, their industrial exploitation between 1917 and 1966 made Makatea one of the economic lungs of French Polynesia at the time. At the height of mining activity, the island was inhabited by nearly 3,000 people, whereas there are now fewer than 100.

Makatea is a jewel like no other. Its plateau, 80m (260ft) above sea level, is mainly covered by primary forest, significantly biodiverse and home to endemic flora and fauna. Apart from the few villagers who venture in to hunt for *kaveu* (coconut crabs), nobody risks entering it. Its countless cliffs, some equipped for climbing, with a *via ferrata* installed in 2019[1], the underwater caves in the heart of the island, its spectacular landscapes, the hospitality of its people and the sites that tell of its recent history make Makatea an unknown jewel, a preserved treasure, and an isolated paradise. Without any proper marine shelter or airport, it can only be visited by boat in fair weather. A few buoys anchored by huge chains – relics of its phosphate mining history – allow small ships to call there. A recently modernized micro-port dug into the top of the reef allows for landing, but it is exposed to the west, prohibiting any stay when there is a strong swell or wind from that quarter.

After a reconnaissance in 2018 that confirmed it would make an interesting addition to DeepHope, we studied Makatea twice, in 2019 and 2021, over an almost 4-km (2½ mile) stretch of the west coast. The reef slopes steeply downwards all around the island. The undulating valleys and spectacular canyons of the reef lead us inexorably down towards the abyss. In the 60–90m zone (c.200–300ft) we find an almost continuous fracture consisting of caves and overhangs that shelter lush flora and fauna, before

1 Makatea Escalade association, Maewan expeditions association, Acropol Tahiti.

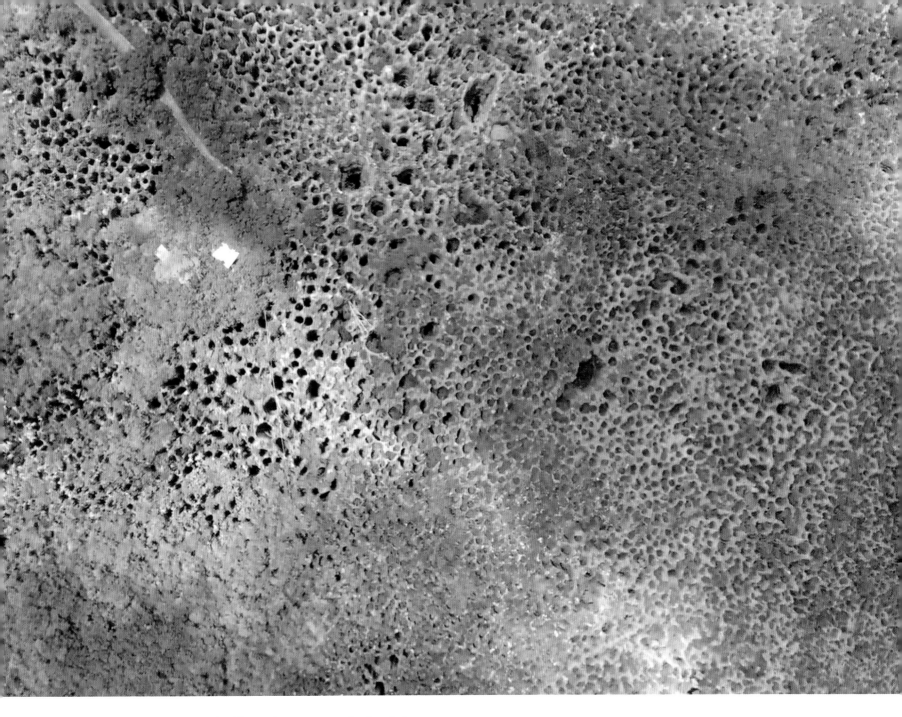

In recent years Makatea's cliffs have become a paradise for climbers from all over the world.

Previous double-page spread: Makatea is a hilly island and it is unique in French Polynesia, whether for its geological characteristics, its biodiversity, its history, or its underwater world. With no airport, no lagoon, and no real harbours, the island is not easily accessible but is nonetheless of great interest.

reaching a steep slope further down, following the classic pattern of reef fronts in the Society and Tuamotu Islands.

Curiously, just as Makatea is different from the other islands, the reef that we found in 2018 is distinctive in a way that we do see nowhere else: it has a substantial covering of *Leptoseris solida*, a coral shaped like large plates that form an exceptionally dense community in the 40–90m (130–300ft) zone. A true field of coral! Why? Is this a local phenomenon or, on the contrary, does it extend significantly further? It is to find out more about it and answer these questions that we return to Makatea in February 2021. Imagine our surprise then, our disappointment even, just 20 months after first studying it, on finding the reef seriously degraded below 30m (98ft). As we start on a hastily adapted scientific programme, our favourite hypothesis involves *taramea*, (the Tahitian name for crown-of-thorns starfish, *Acanthaster planci*). These coral-feeding starfish are indeed capable of wiping out a reef in a matter of months. During our last dive, as we were returning from the seabed, we saw hundreds, maybe thousands, clustering together in the 60–90m (c.200–300ft) zone. We have never seen such an agglomeration of taramea in Polynesia before. The distances they can cover, despite the seemingly negligible speed at which they move, are amazing. Where have they come from? Are they coming up from the seabed, beyond where we can see? What is certain is that this apparently natural episode, together with cyclones and coral bleaching caused by the warming ocean, poses a serious threat to the future of reefs, which have a limited resilience.

The wind turns westerly and it is time to leave Makatea and continue our mission. This is how knowledge is gained, one small step at a time: one day provides answers, another raises new questions.

The caves in the underwater cliff are home to a very rich flora.
They are almost entirely clad in gorgonian corals.

Above, top: The divers begin their ascent from 120m (394ft), with the sun clearly visible on the surface.

Above and opposite: At Makatea, at a depth of 80–90m (260–295ft), we discover a very extensive single-species population of *Leptoseris solida,* with substantial coral coverage and colonies of an unusually large size.

The WHY docked at Tikehau village.

TIKEHAU, THE CAVE OF SHARKS

Apart from Matakea, Tikehau is our first atoll and our gateway to the Tuamotu Islands. Having gone through its pass very carefully (which is necessary because the currents can be violent), we anchor a few miles further south, near the village, in its turquoise lagoon, once visited by Captain Cousteau and his team. Here we go again! As on every island we visit, we carry out a methodical scientific programme here.

For our first working area we choose a site south of the pass, marked by a mooring buoy on the surface. At 60m (196ft) we discover a hole in the reef that looks like the upper opening of an underwater cave. We continue to descend, passing a second hole before levelling off on a steep slope lower down, at 120m (c400ft), at the foot of a cliff where a dark recess attracts us like a magnet. The topography is typical of a classic Polynesian reef but our curiosity is greatly aroused by this apparently large cavity. But time is running out; before we can even consider taking a look on our way back to the surface we have to hurry. While Nico starts on his 40 photoquadrat transect, Julien and I methodically take samples of the corals present at this depth. One by one we put pieces of them into a Ziploc® bag. It is very busy around us: dozens, perhaps even hundreds of grey sharks are roaming the reef! The Bora Bora accident is still fresh in our minds and even though we know that it was quite exceptional and have put it into perspective, none of us looks at these predators in the same way any more. We are constantly aware of them and pay attention to their presence, the way they are swimming, the position of their fins and their behaviour.

We begin our ascent after 20 minutes of diving, going by way of the cave. As we hurry through it, we sense a huge space, even though it is plunged into darkness. Despite the power of our head lamps we can't make out all its walls. We traverse it to the right, going up the slope towards its upper opening, which is accessible by a narrow passage that leads us through a vertical shaft to the exit that we had noticed on our way down. Among the surrounding scree, some greys accompany us in our exploration. It is simultaneously spectacular and mysterious. We had been told about a "cave of sharks" but it was only vaguely described to us. It must be said that, situated as it is between 60–110m (c200–330ft), the few divers who have visited it must generally have done so with classic air-based diving equipment; inevitably, as a result, they were taking a great risk and would have been in a state of nitrogen narcosis incompatible with making fine, precise observations. Thanks to rebreathers and helium-based breathing mixtures, however, we can explore it safely and with clarity. So we find the sharks' cave magnificent and intriguing, but... where are all the sharks? Outside?

Two days later we are back at the foot of the wall to retrieve the sensors and finish the 120m (394ft) scientific protocol. This time we take our underwater camera, the RED. I film Nico and Julien working amid a ballet of grey reef sharks, which are still present in large numbers. It's beautiful and impressive. We always hold a briefing on the surface before these dives. We specify how long each dive will last, everyone's role, the limits and what to look out for and be careful of, so that, once we are submerged, the dive

Loading the equipment onto the 6.60m RIB: the organisation is well practised, with every piece of equipment and person in their place!

The RIB leaves the channel and heads south to
the first study site on Tikehau Atoll. At times it can
take up to 1/2 hours to reach the work areas.

Above: Hundreds of squirrelfish inhabit the Tikehau reef.

Right: At a depth of 110m (362ft), the divers enter the cave. In the 80m zone (260ft) they discover a magnificent chamber that was populated by a large number of grey reef sharks during the divers' second visit. The "shark cave" we had heard about is no legend!

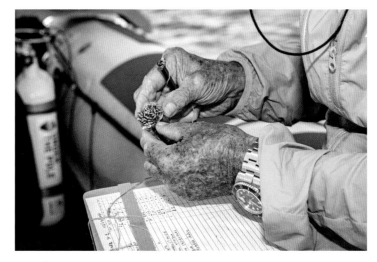

On the RIB, Héloïse is taking samples while Michel starts identifying the corals that have just come up.

proceeds according to a plan that we all know well. This brings efficiency, peace of mind and alertness that help the operations run smoothly. We regularly look each other in the eye. For those who can read them, our eyes can transmit in a fraction of a second the intensity of our emotions such as joy, anxiety or excitement. Here, we are on our guard; personally I feel a little stressed. We venture into the cave in the agreed order: Nico first, followed immediately by Julien, who lights up the wall while I film them from the centre of the cavity. I find myself in near darkness, hidden behind my camera monitor and surrounded by sharks. It's hard to estimate their number but they are everywhere. I see them silhouetted in the halo of the opening or illuminated by my companions' lights as they move forwards. I can feel the sharks around me and I can tell from their attitude that it's not only me who is nervous! It's mind-blowing, we weren't expecting this. I concentrate on framing my camera and continue to move slowly forwards with my thruster. I join Nico and Julien in the light. We share glances that express what we have just been experiencing. A doubt assails me on the way up. I check when we arrive at the decompression station: the last images on my camera were taken deep down, just before we went into the cave. Furious with myself, I realise that, caught up in the action, I had forgotten to press "record" again. I have framed some exceptional images – but without saving them!

We decide to return a few days later, to try to remake the sequence. The same dive, same team, same story, plus strong motivation and a little underlying tension. This time there are not many sharks outside the cave, just one or two patrolling here and there but nothing like the numbers we had seen before. Will there be more inside? Before entering the cave I double-check my camera to make sure that it is recording. There are fewer sharks there today but the sight is still breathtaking. They come and go, accelerating and making energetic changes of direction in front of us, lowering their fins to mark their territory, which we cross without lingering and as discreetly as possible, my legs folded and hidden behind the thruster that is towing me. Coming out of the cave at about 70m (230ft) we encounter a grey shark that is twisting like the Bora Bora one: we emerge quickly, horizontally. We have the film. Even though the sharks had not been swarming so thickly as on our second dive, the images are magnificent and reflect the special atmosphere of the moments we have experienced. A self-contained universe, combining reef diving, deep clear water, a subterranean ambience and a school of sharks.

The three dives that we have made into the cave have allowed us to glimpse its outlines but not to solve its mysteries. Why did we find so many sharks there on one day and so few at other times? We can't connect it with the time of day, the current in or out of the passageway, or the phase of the Moon. Nothing obvious or logical, but the observations were noticeably different on all three occasions. Perhaps one day we will return in an attempt to sketch out some answers to our questions. Surely we, or some other team, will one day come to understand what is happening here that governs the movements of a grey reef shark community around Tikehaku Cave. A mystery that is constantly being repeated at this small point, lost in the middle of the vast ocean...

Héloïse and Gonzalo bring up the net with the last samples
while the divers finish their decompression stop at 6m (20ft).

RANGIROA, MAGICAL TIPUTA

The furiously churning waters of the channel seem to reflect the madness of what is going on below. Only the dolphins leap carefree, showing off to the passers-by and a few tourists on the terrace of the Relais de Josephine. On the bridge of the WHY we too make the most of it. We have been looking forward to this stop on Polynesia's largest atoll. The Tiputa Pass is to diving what El Capitan is to climbing: legendary. A tickbox, I might say, for many divers around the world, sometimes making them irritable when the show doesn't live up to their expectations and reckless when they forget that the outgoing current can easily cause someone who isn't familiar with its ways to be ejected into the open sea. I admire the passionate instructors who, every day, guide teams who have broken open their piggy banks to buy the dive of their lives, receiving radiant smiles when the magic has worked, or bitterness when it was not there. Tiputa is famous for big game fishing. Hundreds of grey reef sharks congregate in the pass – it is reminiscent of strolling along the Champs-Élysées on a Saturday afternoon. It is this concentration that forms the coveted "wall of sharks". Our research sites are always located well away from the passes because they are atypical areas of coral development. Their strong currents mean that only a few species can thrive, which are unrepresentative of the classic coral landscapes of the outer reef slopes. So our scientific programme takes its usual course, although we make sure to explore Tiputa as soon as the opportunity arises. The sharks' indifference, in spite of their abundance, contrasts with the often inquisitive behaviour that they show at greater depths far away from the passes. Since the Bora Bora incident we have been vigilant while working, on the lookout for territorial behaviour, whereas here the sharks move more naturally among the divers.

Our first dive in the pass is a distillation of what it has to offer. We dive at dusk, into the blue[1]. The dolphins that have followed us from the start stay with us for the descent, soon to be joined by some silky sharks and silvertip sharks, *Carcharhinus*

The WHY in the Tiputa channel. With engines at full throttle, it's a question of being vigilant, not dawdling, and hanging on!

albimarginatus, that we normally see at greater depths. During the three and a half hours of the dive we observe a squadron of leopard rays, compact ball-like humpback red snappers, camouflage groupers and huge humphead wrasse or Napoleon fish. We count no fewer than seven different species of shark, including the impressive mokarran (or great hammerhead) and an imposing tiger shark. As the latter approaches the divers out of curiosity, one of the dolphins, apparently regarding us as its own personal entertainment, flaps it away with its tail. The tursiops[2] are extremely entertained by the presence of our cameraman, who moves at a good speed thanks to his scooter. In this submarine jungle, where each creature is by turns hunter and prey, the dolphins move impertinently, seeming to make light of the food needs of the other animals. During the month and a half that we spend on "Rangi" (Rangiroa) we descend as far as 100m (330ft) in the pass, making the most of the rebreathers' advantages to make long forays and discreetly observe the sea life. Always with that famous quotation from Forrest Gump[3] in mind, which can be adapted here: "Tiputa is like a box of chocolates: you never know what you're going to find."

1 To divers, blue indicates that they cannot see the sea floor, often because of its depth.

2 *Tursiops trancatus*, common or Atlantic bottlenose dolphin, a species made famous by the TV series *Flipper*.

3 Original quotation: "*Life is like a box of chocolates: you never know what you're gonna get.*"

Each dive in Tiputa is a marvellous interlude, where we leave
our working tools behind and can fully enjoy the encounters
it provides: manta rays, great hammerheads, or tiger sharks...
Rebreather diving offers us the depth, time and discretion that
allow us to make some high-quality observations of undersea life.

Above: A squadron of leopard rays "flying" over a diver.
Present in the channel in large numbers, their main predator
is the great hammerhead shark.

Right: This pod of bottlenose dolphins lives in Rangiroa. As soon
as we dive in at first light they accompany us to the bottom and
follow us for more than 3 hours, even into the lagoon, keeping
us company during our decompression stops. Their "friendliness"
is astonishing for wild animals: they come into contact with the
divers and put on a show with the greatest of pleasure.

WILD, UNSPOILT RAROIA

"How many times have we failed to notice anything of what life is like in a place? Probably every day. It is our cultural heritage, our social skills that have made us this way and there are reasons and causes for that. But that's no reason not to fight. There are no reproaches, but a certain sadness about this blindness, its scope, and its innocent violence. It is a major challenge to relearn, as a society, to see that the world is populated by entities that are more prodigious than car collections and museum galleries. And to recognize that they require us to transform our ways of life and how we live together."

BAPTISTE MORIZOT, *WAYS TO BE ALIVE*

Kiri and Mako.

Raroia is the third atoll that we visit, after Tikehau and Rangiroa. Compared with the others it is rarely visited and we are impatient to explore its waters. Its underwater topography, its healthy coral and its pass teeming with life seduce us. Many sharks patrol there but the dolphins, less playful and much fiercer than those at Tiputa, keep their distance from us. Chatting in the only small shop in the village, we learn that a *popa'a*[1] couple have been living on a *motu*[11] close to the pass for more than 20 years. The next day we see a small boat heading towards our anchorage. Kiri and Mako, names they adopted when they came to Polynesia, climb aboard, looking forward to meeting us after watching our documentaries. Surprised that they know of us, we ask them about their way of life. Thin and athletic with long, bleached hair, their skin weathered by the sun and smeared with scented *monoï* oil (a Tahitian beauty product), they embody the modern Swiss Family Robinson couple. Because of his love of sea diving Mako had crisscrossed the Tuamotus before settling down on the Raroia *motu*, whose beauty and richness he finds unparalleled. Kiri came to Polynesia in her early twenties to work on an ethnology thesis in Maupiti. Some friends suggested that she should go to meet Mako in Raroia and she never returned. They decided to settle down together and live a simple life, close to nature. Contrary to what one might expect, this did not marginalize them. Almost every day, equipped with a small modem, they go to the far end of the atoll where the reception is good enough to talk to their loved ones and upload the news.

As guests on their *motu*[2], we explore their premises. After several years of sleeping in a tent they finally built a small house that serves as their living space, with one room downstairs and a bedroom above. It is enough to shelter them from the humidity that they had been suffering. A separate shelter serves as kitchen and storage. A workshop a little further away allows Mako to make the magnificent jewellery that he sells to a few passing tourists and to two galleries in Tahiti. Kiri prefers pastels and shows us some of her paintings. Their gardens allow them to supplement the fish that they snorkel for in the pass and they order dry food twice a year to be delivered to the village. But the most amazing thing about Motu Tenukuhaupapatea is the harmony that is evident in the relationship between these two human beings and the nature that surrounds them. They explain that, in the 21 years they have been there, they have created a real Tuamotu bird reserve, where the birds have learned not to fear humans any longer.

To quote them: "*Kirarahu* (white tern)*, goio* (brown noddy)*, kiririri* (black noddy)*, kotiotio* (Tuamotu reed warbler) *and tara* (greater crested tern) *all live here alongside all the migratory birds such as kuriri* (wandering tattler)*, torea* (Pacific golden plover)*, kivi*

---

1 "Foreigner" in Polynesian.

2 *Motu*: small island.

Kiri and Mako, modern Robinson Crusoes for more than
20 years on Motu Tenukuhaupapatea, where they have built
their home in the middle of an almost tame wilderness.

(bristle-thighed curlew), *and kotuku (Pacific reef heron) as well as kurevareva (Pacific long-tailed cuckoo), which are not much liked by the seabirds because they regularly eat their chicks. You can also see large birds such as the frigatebirds, gannets and boobies who call in to rest a while during the day or sometimes spend the night there. More rarely we see koko (atoll fruit dove) and tavake (red-tailed tropicbird) circling over the motu. A colony of kaveka (sooty tern) has found shelter here and is not disturbed when it lays its eggs straight onto the ground, as well as the famous moho (spotless crake), very rare nowadays, which has not even been seen by the old people of the village on Raroia atoll. Because of our love of birds and our closeness to them, we are privileged to count as friends a kotiotio family, a Pacific reef heron and a greater crested tern. This tern, which we call Bella, comes to the roof of our fare (a Polynesian house) every morning to ask for her daily meal, consisting of small sashimi of fish fillet, which she loves. She is always landing on our heads or backs when we are scaling fish, as well as on our hands so that we can stroke her, so strong is our bond of love and trust. Our sacred egret is always present at the feast, sharing it with the many crested terns. As for our little Tuamotu reed warbler, she asks us for cake or a pastry, whistling loudly if we take too long in serving it. For years she has been introducing us to her offspring and every time we adopt and pamper them.”*

At the end of the afternoon they take us to the *motu*'s *ho'a*[3], where they have never hunted with a speargun or fished in any way, in order to preserve its wealth. It is a real aquarium, where marine fauna, unafraid of humans (because they have been totally protected), rub shoulders with sublime corals. We watch the couple feed five camouflage groupers and a triggerfish, as they always do on their way home from fishing. Some *kito*[4], the oldest, tamest ones, allow themselves to be stroked by hand, with palms as well as fingers. We are surprised to see hundreds of *kaveu* (coconut crab) strolling peacefully on the *motu*. They have recently been made a protected species, being in great danger of extinction due to excessive consumption and sometimes unregulated sale. Then Mako shows us the great century-old forest of Tau, home to the atoll's largest colony of black noddies. Apart from a few coconut palms along the pass, the vegetation is totally primitive, "as it would have been at the dawn of creation," say Kiri and Mako.

Yet the couple are preparing to leave their paradise. Rising sea levels and increasingly violent tropical storms indicate that, in a few years, it will no longer be possible to live on the *motu*. They have the opportunity to become guardians of a higher island in the Gambier Archipelago, given to them by a local family.

Kiri and Mako would like the management of their motu to be entrusted to the children of Raroia school, who are already looking after an educational marine reserve. "*Motu Tenukuhaupapatea is an example of wildlife conservation where you can study, all year round, the different nesting phases of birds, as well as observing coconut crabs. The preservation of this natural heritage, the only one of its kind in Polynesia, would offer future generations the privilege and pleasure of observing a protected area of nature and environment. Climate change is more than just a news story in the atolls. This opportunity would allow children to be witnesses, actors and mediators, spreading the word and alerting those people who are not yet aware of the urgency of climate change, while sharing their observations throughout the year.*"

And as if to give a nod in the direction of this wild, almost mystical existence, a whale shark comes to greet the divers who have come for a final dive in front of Kiri and Mako's motu.

3   Channel or pass.
4   Camouflage grouper, also known as blue-tailed cod.

Nico, in the crow's nest, enjoys our arrival in Raroia.
This remote, wild atoll evokes a harmony and gentleness
but it is threatened by rising sea levels.

UNDER THE POLE EDUCATION

EMMANUELLE PÉRIÉ-BARDOUT
Director of Under The Pole expeditions,
sponsor of the Breton eco-delegates

GAËLLE BOUTTIER-GUERIVE
Head of Outreach at Under The Pole

Polynesian children are curious and get caught up in the game of coral identification. Island life is intrinsically linked to the reef and its health.

The IPCC[1] "Special Report on the Ocean and Cryosphere in a Changing Climate" (2019) is the first to highlight the importance of education to improve basic knowledge in the areas of climate change, oceans and the cryosphere (the Earth's frozen zones). Today there is an emerging need for collaboration to develop working practices and concepts that will help us create a more resilient society with greater respect for the ocean.

One of the missions that Under The Pole (UTP) has set for itself is to increase knowledge of undersea ecosystems and polar areas, making scientific findings accessible and understandable to raise awareness and provide education for all age-groups, using resources such as online content, conferences, exhibitions, events etc. as well as through its partnership with the French National Ministry of Education and especially with the education authority of Rennes, Brittany. To achieve this, we provide tools, both real and conceptual, to people who have learnt about the preservation of the oceans and their ecosystems, to help them understand and protect the relevant environments such as the mesophotic zone, polar zones, coral reefs and underwater animal forests.

As well as the work we carry out in schools in mainland France, we naturally continue this mission in the field, during the stopovers of our sailing boat, the WHY.

The knowledge gained by UTP's scientists, as well as the values that UTP embodies – such as curiosity, team spirit, sharing, respect for others and for the environment – are all essential concepts for the protection of nature and for society, which help young people to become agents of change. We promote the ideas in age-appropriate ways, from kindergarten to senior school.

In Greenland, UTP went into schools in several villages and jointly organized, with the Uummannaq children's home, a sled dog expedition on which young people were able to discover the environment in a way that was completely new to them: by diving under the floating ice. They were the first in their community to do so.

The DeepHope and Capsule programmes in French Polynesia, under the aegis of the DGEE[2] and in collaboration with the Polynesian Department of the Environment and CRIOBE[3], have made it possible to educate more than 1,000 students in the main islands

---

1 The Intergovernmental Panel on Climate Change, a group of experts created in 1988 by the United Nations Environment Programme and the World Meteorological Organization, it brings together 195 member states.

2 French Polynesia's General Directorate of Education and Teaching.

3 The Insular Research Centre and Environmental Observatory, a research and service unit of CNRS, the French National Centre for Scientific Research.

(Tahiti, Moorea and Bora Bora) as well as the "remote" islands of other archipelagos (Makatea, Tikehau, Rangiroa, Raroia, Hiva Oa, Fatu Iva, Hao, and Raivavae).

On each island, one or two full days were given over to these presentations by divers and scientists, to thoroughly explain the expedition's objectives and teach the students about their immediate environment, particularly the role of coral reefs and their biodiversity, as well as the threats facing them (climate change, pollution etc.). Each presentation is punctuated by enjoyable practical workshops, such as studying actual coral samples with a magnifying glass, or visiting the WHY, where they are shown the technical equipment that is needed for deep dives. The main objective is to get them to understand human interactions with the ocean and the need for healthy marine ecosystems.

Several schools that are close to an AME (Aire Marine Éducative, Educational Marine Area), where students and teachers can participate in the management of a coastal marine area, have thus been able to increase their knowledge, in collaboration with various other stakeholders such as fishermen, seafarers, local communities, scientists and civil society organizations.

Living as they do in places where climate change is already a reality, young Polynesians, like young Greenlanders, have a particularly intense curiosity and deep interest in the subject, and we hope that these interactions that we have had with them will perhaps lead some of them to think of new career paths.

Faced with the climate emergency and the attack on biodiversity, it is essential that the widest possible public can access a message of awareness and creativity, but also one of hope. At a time when a tiny virus is forcing our world to rethink the way it operates and making it aware of how deeply and directly interconnected we are, during a year when the IPCC has alerted us to both the state of the cryosphere and the risk of coral disappearing by 2050, the planet is reminding us that what is invisible to humans is nonetheless essential. The same is true of the balance of life on Earth.

Humanity has never faced a greater challenge than the one it faces this century, as climatic and social crises converge. Confucius said, *"We are brothers by nature, but strangers by education."* It has never been so urgent for us to bring together education and nature, so that humanity may find its brotherhood. ∎

Emmanuelle shows a primary school class around the WHY.

Héloïse explains the different characteristics of corals to the students.

"They speak of death
as you speak of a fruit
they look at the sea
as you look at a well
the women are lascivious
in the dreadful sun
and there may be no winter
but this is not summer
the rain cuts across
and its every drop beats
some old white horses
that are humming Gauguin
and for want of a breeze
time stands still
in the Marquesas"

Part of Jaques Brel's song "Les Marquises" (The Marquesas),
from his final album (1977)

No lagoon, steep hillsides, we are approaching
the southern islands of the Marquesas archipelago.
This will be our temporary refuge for the cyclone
season and on the DeepHope programme.

Nature in the Marquesas Islands is lush, rich, and fertile: we find tropical fruits and vegetables, which are rarer in the Tuamotu atolls.

THE MARQUESAS

HIVA OA, TAHUATA, FATU HIVA

The festive season, safe from cyclones

A beach of white sand laid flat by the surf, a hut on the shore and the lush green hillsides of the island of Tahuata make an original setting for our Christmas at the end of the world. Garlands hang in the WHY's saloon and in the branches of a beautiful coconut palm that acts as our Christmas tree. The children have made baubles and decorations to add to them. We all take turns to hide away and wrap our presents in secret. A few weeks ago, in Rangiroa, we had a "Secret Santa" draw and each of us pulled out the first name of the person to whom we will give a gift. Tom looks out to sea every so often, having been assured that Father Christmas will arrive pulled by dolphins.

Children and adults alike have played in the rollers for hours today, until sand coats our scalps and scratches our bodies. We are savouring this Swiss Family Robinson life, enjoying the fortnight of rest that we have allowed ourselves after six months of intense work. This picture-postcard anchorage is not, however, typical of the Marquesas, where the few anchorages that exist are rarely sheltered from the rolling sea. From December to March, when we enter Polynesia's risky cyclone period, this is the safest place for sailing boats. Hikes, visits to historic sites and time spent with the local people give us a chance to discover these contrasting

islands that won over and inspired both painter Paul Gauguin and singer Jaques Brel to live here. How can you not be spellbound by the steep cliffs jutting out of the ocean, the wild horses galloping freely, the rocky peaks smothered in lush vegetation, the profusion of fruits, the numerous tiki[1] hidden in the undergrowth like an open-air museum? Here, perhaps more than anywhere else, you can feel the *Mana*[2]. The isolation of the Marqusas and their all-pervading air of wildness have certainly played their part in preserving the authenticity of a culture that was seriously under threat from the colonial administration and the church. The Marquesan people carry their warrior past with them, which one can readily imagine when admiring their magnificent (but

---

[1] *Tiki* in Marquesan, ti'i in Tahitian, a term that also means "man", "god" or "man-god", is a stylized carving representing a human that is found, in Oceania, in the forms of a statue, a tattoo or a pendant, often made from stone, bone or wood.
[2] According to France's CNRTL (National Centre for Textual and Lexical Resources), Mana is a "superior force widespread in nature, inhabiting certain beings and certain things, to which it confers the power to dominate others by their great physical power and almost supernatural gifts, holding both the sacred and the magical and being able to be transmitted to another member of the clan."

Whether pulled by reindeer or dolphins,
Father Christmas always finds his way to the WHY.

A Marquesan from the village of Hapatoni in Tahuata. Tattooing, an ancestral
practice in the Marquesas, almost fell into disuse under the missionaries' ban.
According to Teiki Huukena*, "The symbols that adorned their bodies had a name
and a particular meaning. Some expressed a social rank, an identity, a lineage...
Others a sexual maturity, a personality... Still others, beliefs, local legends...."
Today, these tattoos are considered to be the richest in ancient traditional symbols.

*Author of the books *Hamani Ha'a Tuhuka Te Patutiki* vols I & II,
dictionaries of Marquesan tattooing.

This inlet in Fatu Hiva, originally called the "Bay of Pricks" because of the shape of its pinnacles, was renamed "Bay of Virgins" by 19th century missionaries. We agree with those who claim that it is one of the world's most beautiful anchorages!

plankton. Here, the trade winds blow from the east, lifting powerful seas that crash against the windward cliffs. Mountainous and craggy, with rocky coasts and often impenetrable tropical forests inland, the Marquesas are notorious for being "wild". It's a fair assessment. Below sea level, the difference between this and the other archipelagos of Polynesia is clear: where corals are present despite the absence of a reef, they do not carpet or give structure to the seabed. We will dive no deeper than 67m (220ft) in these waters, the surrounding sea floor peaking for several miles at 60m (c200ft) before sloping away into a region that will remain unknown to us. The Marquesas are renowned for being a home to many pelagic species as well as other more coastal ones, so we continue sampling among manta rays, marbled rays – endemic to the Marquesas – curious silvertip sharks, scalloped hammerheads, grey reef sharks and other silky sharks. Regularly, ever since we began our journey, there have been periodic changes of team members. Some leave us, new ones arrive, old ones return... Departures are always marked by a festive meal tinged with nostalgia, while new arrivals bring new energy on board. Thus we find Romain Pete – a biologist friend who has already been on Under The Pole II – and Aldo, who rejoins us for a few weeks on board the WHY. It is time for Erwan and Emmanuelle to complete their deep diving training, which will gradually allow them access to the 100m (330ft) zone. It is also an opportunity for all the divers on board to have a technical refresher course or a reminder of good practice, most welcome after seven months of diving, with five still to go. In this, Aldo's gentleness, combined with his thoroughness and skill, are just what we need, as the team is sometimes showing signs of tiredness. I have always thought that diving instructors, whose profession makes them – when they embrace their responsibilities with passion – experts in a technical discipline where one is always learning and where humility and the constant questioning of assumptions are guarantees of safety. That is why, every year, we continue to train and retrain. And for that reason, the Marquesas and Aldo's arrival are timely, as we are now halfway through the DeepHope programme.

nonetheless frightening) war-clubs, their proudly tattooed bodies and the *haka*[3] that replaces the more voluptuous dances of the Leeward Islands. And yet, beneath their rougher exterior is hidden the same kindness and sense of welcome that we find throughout Polynesia, like the feast that Jimmy and Pierre lay on for us when they hear that we are leaving Tahuata. That evening, some of the villagers join together around a wild pig that has been hunted especially for the occasion and a huge cake made by our friends for Gonzalo's birthday. The Polynesian people remind me of the Greenlanders. The latter might not be warriors but they share the same "pillars of identity": a spirituality linking Man, objects and elements; powerful craftsmanship; respect for natural resources and careful management of them; the family bond and oral traditions. And when they speak of their land and their ancestors there is something in their eyes and in their posture that gives them the confidence and pride that we have often lost: the link to our roots.

Diving in the Marquesas

While it is said that the Glénan Islands archipelago is Polynesia in Brittany, the Marquesas are Brittany in Polynesia! When you arrive from the Tuamotus, the contrast is striking. We find some turquoise lagoons but in the main the waters are darker, thick with

3   *Haka* means dance in the Marquesan language. This war dance was used to intimidate adversaries during inter-valley conflicts. The tradition is handed on from generation to generation. From an early age, children dance the haka in traditional dress.

Although the waters of the Marquesas are less clear, they are teeming with life. Gonzalo and Héloïse take water samples to analyse the environmental data of the water column at each sampled site.

The WHY moored in the idyllic anchorage of Tahuata, where we spend the festive season. The smallest inhabited island in the archipelago, it has the most coral formations, whereas the others are almost completely devoid of them; this helps to give it beautiful white sand beaches and clear water.

THE GAMBIER ARCHIPELAGO

172M (564FT): EXCEPTIONAL DIVING, FLAWLESS ORGANIZATION

EMMANUELLE PÉRIÉ-BARDOUT: Mangareva, the main island of the Gambiers. The mere mention of its name conjures up dreams, evoking gentleness and tranquillity. These islands, at the eastern end of Polynesia, are truly very remote. Flights from Tahiti are few and it takes a week by sailing boat, making it a rather exclusive destination. There is little tourism, just a few passing sailboats and the occasional supply ship. We lie at anchor for a few days in front of the small village of Rikitea, and have the unexpected opportunity to see Matapukurega 2019, a traditional inter-island festival bringing together the best dancers from the Marquesas, the east of the Tuamotus, the Gambiers, the Austral Islands and even the Easter Island stonemasons. Every evening, dances reverberate and songs ring out, then a magnificent banquet is given, to which everyone is invited. This diversion is very welcome as we are extremely tired after several months of expedition. Michel and Laetitia, who have suspected since the start that the Gambiers could prove rich in discoveries, join us, as well as Gonzalo and Héloise, who are already on board.

GHISLAIN BARDOUT: We have often asked ourselves how far corals grow. Over time, on island after island, we have gained a good knowledge of their diversity, density and distribution on the various sites we have studied. And regularly, out of a diver's curiosity as well as scientific interest, we dived deeper to see where their lowest range might be. According to Michel Pichon's reference sources, the deepest undersea reef-building coral (photosynthetic scleractinian: hard or stony coral) ever observed was at a depth of 165m (541ft), around Johnston Atoll, in western Hawaii. In Rangiroa we noted some below 140m (564ft), and then we collected some at 150m (492ft) in Raroia. Often we will dive a

Searching for deep corals, at 172m (564ft), on a spectacular underwater cliff on the western slope of the Gambiers.

site because of a hunch, like a reconnaissance to verify a hypothesis. When there are more corals than we normally find at 120m (394ft), we suspect we might also find them deeper, as if their depth distribution has shifted downwards. At Raroia, we also noticed that when we travelled slightly sideways at 150m (492ft), the last corals disappeared, suggesting that their presence was part of a vertical "vein".

On 28th March we leave for our first dive in the Gambiers. Probably because the archipelago is so isolated, here at our first site in the west, off the *motu* Tenoko, more than anywhere else, it feels raw and wild, like the end of the world. As if to emphasize this feeling, during our descent, at 95m (312ft) down, we meet a tiger shark coming up from the bottom. At 120m (394ft), the deepest point of the DeepHope programme so far, we have never seen so many corals. While curiously, down to about 30m (c100ft), the reef seems to have been battered by a strong storm swell.

On 1st April, a second dive reaching 140m (564ft) confirms that corals are also present at this depth, and in ways that we have never seen before: *Echinophyllia* as big as plates and smaller Leptoseris. This discovery tempts us to venture even deeper on a third dive.

On 4th April we plan a foray into the zone 170–180m down (558–590ft). We breathe a mixture that our rebreathers make in real time by injecting pure oxygen into a pre-made 4/79 mixture, i.e. composed of 4% oxygen, 79% helium and 17% nitrogen. On the surface, it takes a long time to get ready, what with preparing the mixes, assembling and checking the equipment, briefing, loading the heavy, bulky equipment into our speedboat, navigating to the site…

E. P.-B.: There is a different atmosphere on board this morning. We laughed and joked at breakfast as if to lighten the serious atmosphere that precedes big dives. Then we called together the divers, scientists, surface security and film crew. It's a large group and they all need to know what they have to do to make sure that everything goes according to plan. As the person in charge of safety today, my main concern is to know the precise timing of the dive that Ghislain, Julien and Gaël are about to make. In particular, how many minutes is it likely to be before we see the first parachute arrive on the surface, meaning that the divers have left the very deep zone and that everything is under control. This parameter will define the limits they set for themselves underwater and those that we can collectively accept in terms of safety. After an hour's briefing, we all board the rigid inflatable boat. It takes at least an hour to get to the site. The heat is oppressive but

the conditions are ideal: the water is clear, there's no wind and the sea is flat calm.

G. B.: Once underwater, we relax and regain our peace of mind. This calm also contrasts with the turmoil on the surface. With Julien and Gaël, we regroup on the reef at 20m (66ft) and carry out our final checks before heading for the depths. At 104m (341ft), at the top of an underwater cliff that marks a break with the slope we have just covered, we make one last check. With a look and a gesture of confirmation, everyone signals that everything is fine. We can continue. Shrouded in ever-increasing darkness, we tilt vertically downwards. Crushed by the pressure, our wetsuits become nothing more than thin sheets of neoprene. We regularly inject air into our vests and the gas mix into the "breathing loop" of our rebreathers. We descend: 130m… 140m… 150m (426ft, 459ft, 492ft) and we are still noticing the presence of corals… 160m (525ft)… At 173m (569ft), Julien turns around and stops his descent. We level off beside him and turn towards the cliff wall, as though we are hanging weightless in a vacuum.

Beneath our flippers and behind us there is nothing but blackness. As far down as we can see with our head torches – probably into the 200m zone (66ft) – the drop-off continues. Above us, the water column displays the sumptuous palette of blue that always makes me want to dive this far. At the very top, we can see the top of the drop-off, at 100m (330ft). I like to imagine that since the dawn of time, natural stories have been playing out in these parallel worlds, the oceans, and that at this moment, they are quietly, secretly opening their doors to us.

Here, we live on borrowed time. More than ever, we are exploring the border between two worlds. Although experience, technique and technology allow us to penetrate to these depths, our time here is limited. We have only a few minutes before starting a slow ascent. We scrutinize the wall and there, in front of us, is a coral. Circular, like a flattened dome, it is not large, just a few centimetres in diameter: a *Leptoseris*.[1] We film it next to our depth gauges before picking it up carefully: Laetitia and Michel do not know it yet, but we have just found the deepest photosynthetic scleractinian coral in the world, at -172m (-564ft)!

1   Michel quickly confirmed that the coral collected was a *Leptoseris hawaiiensis*. The findings were published a few months later: Symbiotic associations of the deepest recorded photosynthetic scleractinian coral (172m depth), H. Rouzé, P. E. Galand, M. Medina, P. Bongaerts, M. Pichon, G. Pérez-Rosales, G. Torda, A. Moya, Under The Pole Consortium, J.- B. Raina & L. Hédouin, *The ISME* Journal (2021).

With a signal and a quick, serious, purposeful look at each other we immediately start our ascent, collecting another *Leptoseris* on the fly at -168m (551ft down). At 72m (236ft) below the surface, we slow down and begin our first stops. Our nervous tension abates, we are out of the extreme zone that always makes us tense. We gradually relax, having nothing left to do but wait. We send our samples to the surface and signal to each other that everything is OK. We are happy because we have found the coral we were looking for and because of the journey into the deep that we have just experienced together.

E. P.-B.: We are all watching the water when the red parachute finally appears. We recover it and immediately I take from the net the precious Ziploc® bag containing the samples, which I hand to Michel. With the bag, the divers have put a whiteboard marked "172m" (564ft). Everyone on board is silent as Michel says quietly, "It's a Leptoseris. The record has been broken." There is no arrogance in his words, no pride in a race for the record, simply the statement, and the emotional tears of a 79-year-old researcher who has devoted his life to corals, who has found here new answers to the questions he had long been asking himself.

It is quite a personal achievement for us all, but for him, at the end of a career that has lasted almost 60 years, this sample has a different meaning. After 4 hours and 8 minutes of diving, Ghislain, Julien and Gaël emerge on the surface. In the warm orange evening light we welcome them, with wide smiles on our faces and thumbs up to confirm their success! Their faces, though, are tired; they look as though they have returned from a long journey. Today, the effort, the group cohesion and the combination of different skills have shown that we can push back the limits of scientific exploration. Above all, as Laetitia emphasized: *"This calls into question our entire vision of the reef and how it functions, because today, we can no longer ignore these deep ecosystems and their contribution to the functioning of the reef."*

Collecting a *Leptoseris hawaiiensis* at 172m (564ft), and much excitement on the surface for Michel who identifies it as the deepest photosynthetic mesophotic scleractinian coral in the world.

DEEP-SEA CORALS, A NEW DIMENSION TO BE TAKEN INTO ACCOUNT

DR LAËTITIA HÉDOUIN
CNRS Research Fellow
at the Centre for Island Research
and Environmental Observatory - CRIOBE -
(USR 3278 EPHE CNRS PSL)

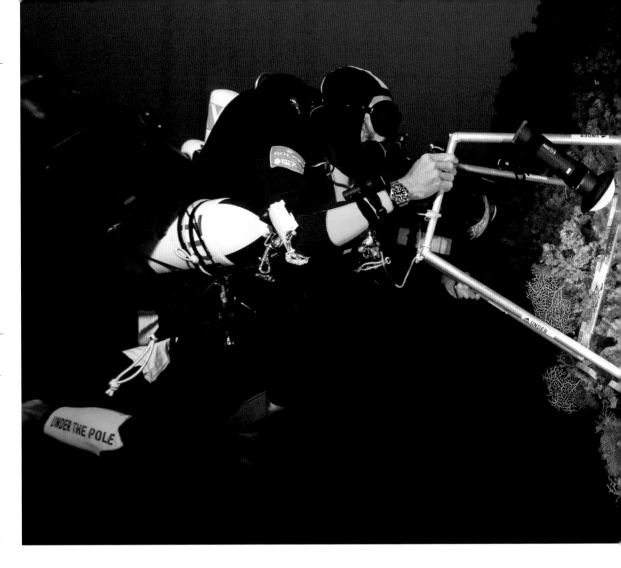

Coral reefs are noted for their clear waters, their corals and an unparalleled diversity of multicoloured fish. They are built by the coral, an incredible animal that lives in symbiosis with microalgae called zooxanthellae.

This symbiosis allows coral to proliferate in oligotrophic waters1: the microalgae, through photosynthesis, provide it with up to 95% of the energy it needs. Because the microalgae depend on light for photosynthesis, it was long believed that reef-building corals only colonized the surface waters.

Recent discoveries, however, have revealed unexpected results. Living corals can be found beyond a depth of 30m (98ft); some are species that also live on the surface, but there are certain species that are specific to the depths of the reef. This zone between 30 and 165m depth (98–541ft) is the mesophotic zone, also called the Mesophotic Coral Ecosystems (MCEs). In French Polynesia we discovered that photosynthetic scleractinian corals (or reef builders) are capable of living to 172m (564ft). This, the record depth observed during the DeepHope research programme, demonstrates corals' ability to acclimatize to environments with extremely limited light.

1 A particularly nutrient-poor environment.

Less than 1% of surface light reaches the 170m zone (558ft), yet some species of photosynthetic scleractinian corals colonize these depths. Exploration of these mesophotic reefs from 30 to 172m (98–564ft) across the five Polynesian archipelagos has led to many unsuspected discoveries. For example, certain species were found to be present in geographical areas where they had never been recorded before, probably because past inventories were mainly conducted at the surface.

The other surprise is that the diversity and richness of coral genera reaches a maximum in the 40–60m zone 130–196ft), whereas coral cover generally decreases with depth.

Furthermore, analyses carried out on the 11 islands show that coral communities become increasingly different with depth. While coral landscapes are relatively similar at the surface in the islands studied, a high diversity of coral landscapes is observed in the deep zone, revealing the uniqueness of these mesophotic landscapes. These findings and the unique features of these deep reefs should be taken into account in conservation and protection measures to represent the diversity of coral habitats in French Polynesia. If the mesophotic zone between 30 and 60–80m (98 and 196–260ft) has so-called generalist corals, i.e. corals that live both at the surface and in the

depths, the deeper zone of the mesophotic reefs located between 60–80 and 170m (196–260 and 558ft) is a special zone where only certain corals are able to live. Indeed, compared with the so-called upper zone (between 30–60m/98–196ft), light levels are even more limited, and only a few coral species have developed mechanisms to live in these extremely poorly lit environments. If the deep zone of ECMs is populated by a particular diversity, it is part of the richness of the biodiversity of coral reefs, and it is important today to consider the reef in three dimensions, and not only two, as was done for many years. Depth is a criterion that can no longer be neglected in

the management and conservation of reefs, because mesophotic ecosystems are simply an extension of those on the surface and they make up the coral reef together. ∎

Divers take a series of photoquadrats at different working depths. It will take months to process the thousands of images to compare the diversity and coral cover of the mesophotic reefs with those of the surface.

THE AUSTRAL
ARCHIPELAGO

RAIVAVAE

A few degrees cooler, appendicitis and losing a RIB

Sitting under the dodger[1], I've been staring at the stern of the WHY for the past three hours. Behind it, the mooring line of the 6.6m RIB (21ft 8in rigid inflatable boat) is getting tauter and tauter as each new breaker hits. With waves 4m (13ft) high and 30–35 knot winds (341/2–40mph), the crossing from the Gambier Islands to the Austral archipelago is tough. We're travelling with the surf, regularly making 13 knots (15mph). It wouldn't be unpleasant if I weren't now certain that we will lose our work dinghy in a matter of a few hours. There are still three days to go and neither the wind nor the sea is likely to ease off. Although we have used tyres as shock absorbers and attached five hawsers, we are reaching the limits of this set up. It will not hold. Two hawsers have already failed. Several times we struggle to replace them but we're reaching the limits of what can be done. Towing the 6.6 has been our pet peeve since the beginning, but it's a compromise that is essential for the logistics of the dives because the WHY's deck is too small for us to carry it on there. We have always managed to sail in windows of decent weather but as we move further south and the southern winter sets in, the conditions are rougher and we can do nothing about it.

At the change of watch, Ghislain and I agree not to try to rescue the RIB when the last hawser fails. We have weighed up all the possible options and nothing is feasible without taking undue risks. A few hours later, the last hawser snaps and in dismay we watch our dinghy drift away. The crew members are perplexed by our apparent fatalism but they soon realise how dangerous a rescue attempt would be. Two and a half days later, we arrive by night in the Raivavae channel. The "landing" is tense, one of our two engines is defective, the wind is strong, the map does not match the markings in the channel. When leaving, in daylight, we notice that the GPS position is wrong by several hundred metres. Someone is put on watch at the bow. The WHY's searchlight, originally installed to spot icebergs, comes in very useful. The mainsail jams as it is being lowered and I have to climb the boom to help it down. Finally we enter the lagoon and can breathe more easily. The crew is made up of more divers than sailors, but after eight months it is clear that they have gelled into a reliable team, everyone knows how to stick to their post and concentrate on the steering when necessary.

1   Protective cap around the helm station.

Arriving at Raivavae, in the Austral Islands, in a strong wind.
To get through the channel, a crew member watches over
the bow with a VHF lamp to warn of potential dangers.

The team on the peak of Mount Hiro, at 438m (1,437ft), the highest point of Raivavae, offering an exceptional panorama.

Located 630km (392 miles) from Tahiti, the island of Raivavae is the southernmost destination in our programme. Mount Hiro is volcanic and reaches an altitude of 438m (1,437ft). The climate, cooler than in the rest of Polynesia, is suitable for growing vegetables and we put on our jumpers and jackets for the first time in a long while! Ghislain complains of increasingly intense stomach pains. Antoine, the nurse on board, contacts our previous doctor, Emmanuel, who thinks it is appendicitis. They decide to put him on antibiotics while he returns to Tahiti and operate if the diagnosis is confirmed. And that's how it turns out: Ghislain is "relieved" of his appendicitis in the hospital in Papeete, a few weeks later! In the village, we meet a fisherman who agrees to hire us his services on his potimarara, a local fishing boat, so that we can dive at sea, as we no longer have our RIB. The water, like the air, is cooler and so we add our shorties[2]. We also reduce the duration of the dives by about 30 minutes for greater comfort and safety. Underwater, the slope is gentler and pinnacles, cavities and canyons punctuate the sea bed's surface. Galapagos sharks replace grey sharks. Because of its remoteness, this island has been little studied and we collect coral species that we have not sampled elsewhere, including one that is a new find for Polynesia.

Before leaving, some of us climb Mount Hiro while others take a break from the daily grind in the islet's swimming pool on the most beautiful *motu* we have visited so far. Alone in the world, we revel in the place's tranquillity before returning to the bustle of Tahiti.

2   Short-sleeved, knee-length diving suit.
In this case, we put them on over our full-body suits.

The samples collected during DeepHope form the largest collection of mesophotic corals in the world.

THE FINAL CURTAIN

LAST DIVE

At a depth of 6m (20ft), my computer indicates 72 minutes before I return to the surface. I have just returned from 120m (394ft), a depth I would never have thought I would reach a few months ago. I look over at Erwan, for whom this is also a first. He is photographing the coral colonies we have been studying for months. This dive was great from start to finish, the long descent by thruster, working on the seabed at 120m (394ft) in such a special atmosphere, the caves, a visit by an albimarginatus shark and now the transparent waves that we can see crashing on the reef above us.

We are back in Moorea and, as they say, "we have closed the circle." Laetitia has asked us to do two dives to compare the condition of the reef after almost a year and an episode of coral bleaching. In a fortnight the team will go their separate ways for the month of July before meeting again in Moorea in a month's time. A certain sense of nostalgia, full of happiness and pride, comes over me: this study of mesophotic corals has been a success. We have achieved our objectives and the results are beyond all our expectations. Scientists now have the largest collection of mesophotic corals in the world, we have brought back, from 172m (564ft) down, the deepest hard coral (photosynthetic scleratinia) ever seen and collected in the world, we have reported species new to Polynesia and to science… Above all we hope that this study and the ones to come will make it possible to adopt

measures to conserve these refuge zones, a ray of hope for the coral reefs that are bleaching and dying around the world, which is a colossal loss for the biodiversity of the oceans[1].

And now the long laboratory work will begin, analysing and processing all the data generated by the expedition: analysis of thousands of photoquadrats, of the samples' genetics, of the acoustic data recorded by the hydrophones, of the oceanographic measurements picked up by the sensors placed at different depths and the analyses made at each site along the water column. Our scientists have a few years of work ahead of them!

As is often the case, I only realise at the very end of the mission just how great a challenge we had taken on. Living and working with twelve, sometimes fifteen people on board the WHY, steadily increasing the number of deep dives while doing demanding work, going from one island to another and one dive site to another, dealing with inflating tanks and mixing gases, maintenance and repairs, taking samples in the swell and in the blazing sun, often until nightfall, processing photos and videos, organising the filming of the documentary, making frequent long

1   In September 2019, an IPCC report supports the alarm raised by scientists, stating, among other things, *"By 2050, all coral species in tropical regions will have disappeared almost completely"*.

The final dive, where it all began, in Moorea.
From 140m (459ft) down, the entire cliff is visible.
For a short time, the divers are in a real parallel world.

voyages in weather that is too calm or too rough, and doing the washing up (!)... but above all making sure that harmony continues to reign on board while everyone is working hard and tiredness takes an ever-greater toll on us as time goes by. Fortunately, the essential evening aperitif and occasional parties keep this camaraderie alive, with always more stories to be told. Even Tom and Robin, aged 3 and 7, have found us out and want to join in with the evening drinks! I smile into my mouthpiece as I think of my two beloved blond boys who, having grown up mostly in the Arctic, have now discovered the joys of warm waters. Robin swims and dives like a fish and I kept the promise I made him three years ago: we went swimming with great whales together. Tom jumps off the WHY like a cork; fearless, he is really funny but equally he can be a pain. With his lisp, he tells anyone who will listen that he is a "surfer, but especially a sportsman!" Although it hasn't always been easy for the boys to have to put up with such a small space to play in the boat's saloon, surrounded by our tons of equipment, the WHY team have all become members of our two children's family, hugging them, reading stories, playing and colouring, buttering their toast for them in the morning, even punishing them sometimes. Most of the team are young and have no children, and even if they are sometimes annoyed by a new mistake, their kindness and patience are (almost) limitless. Camille, the boys' 26-year-old nanny, who left France at the same time as I did, 16 months ago, has played a big part in this delicate balance between our professional and family lives. And she herself has changed so much! Having embarked on this adventure without ever having lived at sea, or even sailed on a boat, she has not only adapted to our way of life, but has become an incredible crew member on the ground, taking the children to a *motu* in a RIB by herself, jumping off the boat with Robin and Tom, sharing Robin's education with me, cooking small meals for everyone's delight, overcoming her seasickness during the voyages... She even successfully passed her level 1 diving course among the dolphins and sharks of Rangiroa.

Everyone on board the WHY has contributed to this mission's success. On board, we are not just divers, technicians or photographers, we are "crew." This title reflects the spirit that Ghislain and I want to instil, one that does not pigeonhole everyone by their speciality. On the contrary, success depends on the ability of each person to listen to the other, to take over when a friend is tired. While Ghislain and I are the project leaders, everyone on the

Team photo in Rangiroa.

team has taken ownership of the project and made the mission a success. DeepHope was certainly the biggest and most demanding of all the science programmes that Under The Pole has been involved in. Even more than the challenge it represented in terms of diving, we all realised this programme's importance and the hope it represents for coral reefs. Our view of these ecosystems, so essential to the biodiversity of the oceans that we love so passionately, has changed. We will continue to study reefs in the coming months. Something tells me that we will always return to this subject from now on, because, while the polar regions have a strong attraction for us, the study of reefs and the fragile balance that they represent is equally captivating and there is still so much to discover in the mesophotic zones!

I look at my computer, which indicates only a few minutes of decompression stops remaining. I take advantage of these last moments between two worlds. When I get my head out of the water, Robin or Tom will surely be there to ask me a question as if I had just come back from shopping, those who remained on board will greet me with smiles and ask how the dive went, the scientists will ask if the harvest was good and I will ask them ask if we have found anything new... I will miss it all, but also, after all these years, I know that this is not the end. You must finish one mission in order to start another. And in a month's time, there will be more of us than ever in Moorea to carry out the Capsule programme.

The house and the pontoon for loading and unloading

CRIOBE (Centre for Island Research and Environmental Laboratory)

A YEAR OF COLLECTING, AND NOW WHAT?

DeepHope is over. Like any story, it had to come to an end. And so, after 12 months of criss-crossing Polynesia, sailing from island to island at breakneck speed, diving day after day to depths of 120m and sometimes beyond (400ft or more), this exceptional programme is over. Or the field part of it at least, since the resulting analyses and publications will take years.

For those who experienced it, DeepHope will always be an extraordinary programme, one of those that we dream about, that make us grow and that we will remember fondly. It is not every day that one experiences such an adventure: its scientific interest and quality, its duration, its geographical coverage, the amount of technical equipment used, its complex logistics and in particular the repetition of extreme dives, make DeepHope a remarkably successful major mission. A challenge, or rather a set of considerable challenges, which had to be met with rigour, humility and patience.

As mentioned previously, when we prepare an expedition and then carry it out in the field, questions nag at us on a daily basis, crushing us under the weight of the associated responsibilities: how do we make sure that everything goes well? How can we meet the challenges we have set ourselves without accidents? How do we avoid the irreparable? But above all, the most important thing is to keep the team safe. This is of prime importance on expeditions such as Under The Pole, where commitment has always been the order of the day. DeepHope presented particularly complex risks. It is often said that nothing is impossible, but when faced with an inexact science such as decompression physiology, how do you repeat deep dives at a sustained rate, safely, over a very long period of time and with many divers? How do you reconcile the ambitions and wishes of a diverse team of enthusiasts and experts? Answering these questions has been DeepHope's biggest challenge. Over the months, miles, and dives, everyone on board has drawn on hidden reserves of personal strength to face their responsibilities and maintain an almost family atmosphere on board, which, in the close confines of an expedition yacht, is both an obligation and a challenge. Everyone accepted the rules, played the game and complied with the high demands of a programme of excellence.

Scientifically speaking, DeepHope is the biggest programme we have ever done with Under The Pole. It demonstrates the value of combining expertise to advance the limits of scientific exploration. Laetitia Hédouin's research team could never have carried out the dives we did, just as we could never have carried out the in-depth study that they envisaged. But together we have just completed one of the largest studies of deep corals ever conducted in the world. An example of successful collaboration and a model for the future – in our view – that inspires us and which we hope to replicate in future.

We now have a better understanding of how important coral reefs are for the planet, these oases of life that, like the tropical forests on land, are home to 30% of the biodiversity of the oceans. As we dived, descending into the intoxicating blue of the depths, or spent long periods of time just a few metres below the surface, we became more curious. Why did we discover such a large expanse of *Leptoseris solida* corals at 90m (295ft) on the Makatea reef? Why, at 120m (394ft) in the Gambiers, did we find more species, of greater size and in larger numbers than anywhere else? Why, deeper down at the same site, did we find a *Leptoseris hawaiiensis* coral at 172m (564ft), making it the deepest reef-building coral in the world? Some of the observations we were able to make have raised new questions. Yet the high standard of the programme, the rigour with which it was carried out and, ultimately, the quantity of scientific data brought back will provide answers, of course. Above all it will bring us detailed new knowledge of the important role of deep coral reefs, leading to a better understanding of them, knowledge that can provide a sound basis for their preservation.

DEEPHOPE I & II, REVIEW AND OUTLOOK

DR LAËTITIA HÉDOUIN
CNRS Research Fellow
Centre for Island Research and Environmental
Observatory - CRIOBE -
(USR 3278 EPHE CNRS PSL)

The DeepHope I and II research programmes carried out in French Polynesia on mesophotic reefs laid foundations, bring the first on this subject in the French overseas territories. They made it possible to discover coral reefs, through the study of ECMs (Mesophotic Coral Ecosystems), on twelve French Polynesian islands (Moorea, Bora Bora, Tahiti, Makatea, Tikehau, Rangiroa, Raroia, Tahuata, Hiva Oa, Fatu Hiva, Mangareva and Raivavae) between 6 and 120m deep (20–394ft). Having collected a total of more than 6,000 samples through DeepHope I, we have found evidence of species that are new to French Polynesia and discovered corals' great ability to colonize the mesophotic zone, as well as noting the surprising diversity of coral communities in the 40–60m zone (130–196ft).

DeepHope has made it possible to amass the largest collection of mesophotic corals in the world, with a total of 2,169 samples collected between 6 and 172m (20–564ft), and 1,749 samples of mesophotic corals, from below 30m to 172m (98–564ft), belonging to 43 coral genera. Over and above the diversity of the species listed, this has made it possible to understand how coral landscapes change with depth, and to discover areas with a surprising overlap. Life in ECMs is constrained by limited light conditions, and coral cover decreases with depth, from 40% at the surface (6m/20ft) to less than 3% at 90m depth (295ft). However, certain geographic areas contradict this trend. Atypical coral landscapes have been discovered, for example at 120m (394ft) in Mangareva, where the coral cover reaches 30% thanks to the presence of lamellar corals of the *Montipora genera*. In Makatea, the 90m reef (295ft) is mostly dominated by pink lamellar *Leptoseris solida* and in Raroia, the 40m reef (130ft) reaches 79% coral cover because of the dominance of *Pachyseris speciosa*. These results show that certain deep areas of the reef allow the development of abnormally prolific coral populations. Although the reasons for this coral proliferation still remain unknown today, it reveals the importance of these ECMs in the biodiversity of reefs.

DeepHope has also led to understanding how the so-called generalist corals, i.e. those capable of living both in the surface zone (6m/20ft) as well as in the mesophotic zone (beyond 40m/130ft), were able to adapt to this decrease in light and therefore to the potential energy limitation. The strategy used by *Pocillopora verrucosa*, commonly called the "cauliflower" coral because of its surface shape, is to decrease with depth the number of polyps per surface (to limit its energy needs) and also to flatten out its skeleton shape to enable improved light collection. This transformation of coral skeletons has already been observed in a few other areas of reef, but confirms the plasticity of corals to environmental changes.

DeepHope I raised many questions about how Polynesian ECMs function, and DeepHope II, conducted over a year later, provided additional information on these distinctive, under-studied ecosystems. Initially, one of the main objectives of DeepHope II was an

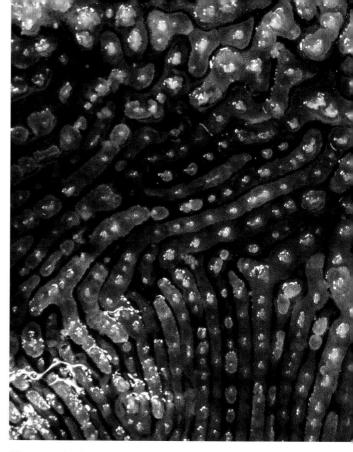

Close-up of a Cycloseris wellsi, commonly found at a wide range of depths.

in-depth study of the Makatea reef, due to the presence of the *Leptoseris solida* field detected during our first reconnaissance trips in 2018 and 2019. Unfortunately, much to the surprise of the Under The Pole team, the coral field was found to be mainly dead due to a proliferation of thorny starfish, known as "*taramea*" (the Polynesian name for *Acanthaster* starfish). More than 70% of the colonies of *Leptoseris solida* have been devoured by the *taramea*, leaving a veritable underwater cemetery in place of the coral field discovered two years previously, and this in a few months. This catastrophic observation demonstrates that even the mesophotic areas are affected by these biological blooms, and are not spared, despite being located lower down in the reef. Another atypical coral field having been detected in Moorea, some of the research efforts were redeployed there to study and categorize

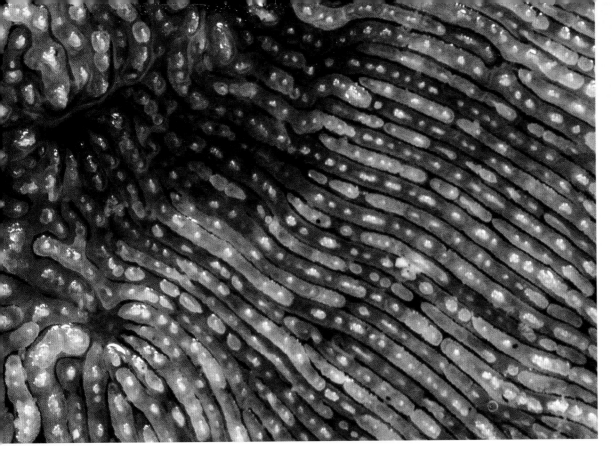

Laëtitia Hédouin, director of the DeepHope programme, 2018–2021.

this site, which is composed mainly of flat rose-shaped coral colonies of *Porites rus* in the 25–45m zone (82–148ft), with a coverage of more than 50%.

Finally, a critical piece of information for coral reef management emerging from DeepHope was to discover that coral bleaching had more impact at the surface than at depth. While 30% of the colonies were affected by the 2019 bleaching in Moorea in the 6m zone (20ft), fewer than 8% were affected from 40m deep (130ft). The 30–60m zone (c100–200ft) could therefore constitute a climatic refuge for the species found there. It is essential to take these data into account in future reef protection measures, because this mesophotic zone between 30 and 60m zone (c100–200ft) could therefore provide a natural conservatory of corals in the face of climate change.

Deep reefs remain under-studied and the results provided by DeepHope I and II help to provide a better understanding of their role, their diversity and their functioning in French Polynesia. Programmes now being initiated for the long-term monitoring of these particular environments may play a critical role in the future. While scleractinous corals were DeepHope's main target, many other animals have been seen to colonize the depths of the reef, including black corals and gorgonians. They could play a similar role by creating ecosystems called "underwater animal forests". In recent years these have been arousing a growing interest because they can create oases of life in the middle of depopulated areas; these animal forests, of which coral reefs are one of the best known examples, exist in all the oceans, from the polar zones to tropical areas. However, their functioning, diversity, role and fragility remain poorly understood.

It is in this context that we have set up, jointly with Under The Pole, a new research programme, DeepLife. Today it is essential to study these exceptional areas of biodiversity and their vulnerability to climate change, with the aim of providing the information that managers and politicians need to put in place the conservation, adaptation and mitigation measures that are required to protect underwater animal forests. ∎

CAPSULE PROJECT

AUGUST
TO NOVEMBER 2019

THE ORIGIN

This is the story of a time when anything seemed possible, when underwater exploration and space exploration were carried out side by side, two conquests with so many similarities, both of them so inspiring for humanity. For a long time I had believed that everything had been done; however...

For years I have thought nostalgically about that period from the 1950s to the 1990s, the heyday of the pioneers who "industrialized" ocean exploration. Those were the days of Cousteau's Odyssey and the underwater adventures of his German counterpart, Hans Haas, the first undersea houses, the COMEX adventure of Henri-Germain Delauze or Jacques Piccard's quest into the abyss on board his bathyscaph. Together with Émile Gagnant of Air Liquide, Cousteau had invented the first regulator, a revolutionary breathing apparatus that would allow man, following in the wake of Commander Cousteau's Calypso, to dive in all latitudes for almost 40 years. Stopovers on the seabed became more frequent and lasted longer. It seemed that mankind could live beneath the sea. Nitrogen may have restricted access to the depths because it induced narcosis, but so what! It was replaced, first by helium and then by hydrogen, pushing ever further the limits of neurotoxicity that are linked to the solubility of these inert gases. In the 1960s the largest programmes began, with Precontinent I, II and III, that were aimed at making it possible to stay undersea for long periods. Saturation diving was born, and was simultaneously industrialized by COMEX, the Compagnie Maritime d'Expertises. We went from undersea houses to the concept of saturation diving bell, operated from the surface by ships, with control stations worthy of any space capsule. An ambitious submarine programme (SAGA), allowing divers to work at several hundred metres' depth, was even started by Cousteau before being taken over by COMEX and IFREMER, then abandoned in 1990 following a record dive off Monaco. In 1988, with the COMEX Hydra VIII programme, humankind showed it was possible to work at –534m (1,752ft) during an experimental dive in the Mediterranean. And 2 years later, on Hydra X, Italian diver Theo Mavrostomos reached the unbelievable record depth of –701m (2,300ft) during a simulated hyperbaric chamber dive. I have often said to myself that I should have been born one or two generations earlier so I could have been a part of it: I would have sailed on the Calypso, dived on board the "Diving Saucer" beside Albert Falco, accompanied Hans Haas in his round-the-world adventures to tell of the discovery of a new world,

experimented with diving bell to explore the limits of the human body. But no, I was born in 1980, and at the time that my mind and body were being moulded, it was already too late: the Berlin Wall was falling, the world was changing and 40 years of unprecedented human underwater exploration ceased. It was the end of an era, an end to the apparent recklessness of the pioneers, as their romantic quest faded into a new age: that of the robots. Mankind seemed to have reached its limits and machines would now take over, relegating humans to missions less prestigious than exploring their own limits and the deep.

In the early 2000s, after half a century of human underwater exploration, what was left for us? How could we satisfy our appetite for exploring the depths when our forefathers seemed to have done everything already?

Today a few veterans survive from that era: a few pioneers and their heirs. All have one common trait, one that I share myself: their eyes shine with the same passion, the same love of adventure and discovery. I love watching them tell me of their lives and their exploits, like grown-up children remembering a time when anything was possible. Whilst filled with nostalgia for the experiences they have had, they nonetheless admit, almost with a tinge of regret, that no, not everything has been done before. So there is, still, a window of opportunity on the horizon, a gap in our knowledge for 21st century explorers to exploit, thanks to a forgotten 19th century diving suit that has gradually been gaining new momentum since the 1990s: the rebreather.

Even in high school I was already dreaming about deep diving and the potential of rebreathers. At that time marine biologist Richard Pyle wrote about these suits and their potential for exploring reefs below a depth of 60m (c200ft). These were the days of the first tentative steps, when cavers such as Olivier Isler were developing prototypes that pioneers hailed as a tool to revolutionize human underwater exploration in self-contained suits. And indeed, since its inception it has pushed all the limits of scuba diving, setting an impressive number of records. Yet, most importantly, it has opened a window into a new area with enormous potential. Now a diver can make much longer forays than before, accessing greater depths more easily. It is a superb tool for discovering the marine environment. But now, how can we reach even further? How can we push back the limits of time or depth, without the danger of falling into the tedious, complex process of saturation diving as it is usually done?

The Saga submarine in its
hangar in l'Estaque, Marseille.

GENÈSE

How can one innovate in underwater exploration? How push aside some of the limits that stand in the way of human ingenuity? How shall we push back the frontiers of human knowledge? What do we know how to do, what are our strengths, and what are our limits? How can we make a difference and contribute to the quest for knowledge? We mulled over these questions for a long time before embarking on the programme of undersea living that would become Capsule.

We started from the basis that a scuba diver equipped with a rebreather and underwater scooter or thruster is an optimal set-up for exploratory diving. Although the kit may, in time, be miniaturized and made more reliable, it appears that humans have reached their physiological limits and will realistically never dive much deeper, or for longer, than they already do, unless we reconsider saturation diving, developed in America and then in Europe from the 1960s. To stay underwater for long periods, not for assembling oil or gas pipes but to study the ocean from within, with no time limit. It is Jules Verne's dream! And also the dream of a cohort of explorers, from yesterday and today, whose more or less crazy ideas have marked out this long history of feats and dramas, all with a single goal: to live under the sea.

In the spring of 2016 we too decided to set out on this path, putting our time and energy into an undersea habitat project, to advance scientific knowledge. Just as one cannot imagine it would be possible to sum up the entire terrestrial kingdom from a few hours' observation, time spent underwater is key to understanding the submarine environment. This belief would, like a pathway, lead an idea to grow within us...

But how shall we innovate in a world where costs quickly become prohibitive and where so much has already been done? I have long dreamt of a modern-day Nemo, a submarine able to offer a panoramic view of the depths, sending its teams of divers out to explore the coasts of the world. But between the web-footed biped equipped with a diving suit and a scientific "spit-diver" submarine[1], there is a dizzying quantum leap. So we opted for our first saturation diving experience to be at an intermediate level, while still having its share of innovations.

The development, construction, transport and running costs would have to be reasonable and need only a small team. We also wanted it to be environmentally friendly, self-supporting in gas and energy for three divers over a period of one to three days, and as discreet as possible. The complete system should fit into a 20-foot container and thus be able to be moved quickly from site to site with standard lifting equipment. As well, of course, as being operable from the WHY with Under The Pole's own equipment. In short, it should be simple, uncluttered, relatively autonomous, economical and ecological, easy to transport and quick to deploy: a few challenges were looming on the horizon and we would certainly have to be innovative. These specifications were not those of a deep saturation diving base, which require days, if not weeks, of decompression – and therefore enormous budgets. The idea was for an underwater shelter to be positioned somewhere close to the surface, probably in the 12–25m zone (40–82ft), in order to guarantee the divers' maximum safety and particularly their return to the surface within a few hours. An underwater tent, the "pop-up tent" of the seas! A survival shelter that lets divers avoid returning to the surface at the end of their excursions, but to protect themselves instead, to return to normal gravity and the landmarks of land dwellers, to be able to sleep and eat, yet still contemplate the deep. Underwater camping is what we were planning to do, but hi-tech camping! At last I have got the right idea, directly inspired by Himalayan climbing equipment. For in their quest for the heights, Himalayan climbers generally have to shelter in a series of advance camps between their base camp and the point that they are aiming for. These precarious shelters make human life and survival possible in a hostile environment during climbers' forays into the planet's highest altitudes. Although the undersea environment is very different, the philosophy is similar: our underwater "tent" would provide divers with the essential shelter for them to satisfy their quest, not for great depths so much as for enough time to extend their stay in the heart of the ocean.

The idea was there; it was now necessary to give it shape. Since the concept was to make something like a tent, that is what we started to design: a transparent bubble, simultaneously flexible and durable. But this romantic, harmonious and deeply inspiring vision was not realistic enough to match our specifications

---

1 A submarine consisting of one zone at atmospheric pressure and another at ambient pressure, allowing divers to exit.

and was incompatible with the technical constraints and our concerns about strength and durability. Our artistic vision was forced to confront an engineer's realism. We continued to draw shapes, jot down ideas and play with volumes. Whenever we met to exchange ideas and compare our sketches, new problems and solutions appeared. Little by little the project came to life.

At the same time we started to consider the problems of saturation *per se*. The specifications for our shelter would mean having to decompress in the water, and in order to develop a protocol that would suit a number of different individuals we decided to limit its duration to a few hours. This was the beginning of a thought process that our working party followed for almost three years. We began discussing the strengths and limitations of our approach with Jean-Éric Blatteau, a diving doctor, and diving physiologist Julien Hugon. In the course of our discussions – sometimes alarming, sometimes inspiring – we set out on a path where the science was not always certain, navigating a course between published research, the temptation to experiment, responsibility and reason. I then approached Jean-Marc Belin, a decompression expert, who had managed Laurent Ballesta's 24-hour dive. His innovative approach had significantly reduced Ballesta's decompression time: food for thought. In January 2017 I met Bernard Gardette, former scientific director of COMEX, at the company's headquarters in Marseille. We didn't know each other and, uncertain what to expect, I almost felt intimidated. My way there, between buildings and through gardens dotted with diving bells and all kinds of other exploration devices, was a pilgrimage in itself. How would he receive the ideas that I was about to present to him? Well, it was simple and exciting. I met someone incredibly positive, who was open and attentive to my ideas and whose gaze reminded me of those of the pioneers. From then on, we exchanged ideas more often, the first simulations came out and we began to build a decompression model that would evolve as our habitat was developed.

In the summer of 2017, as we sailed through the Northwest Passage for the first stage of Under The Pole III, with time running out, we forgot about our designs and protocols for the time being. We returned to them with Sylvain Pujolle, the UTP team's engineer, and joined by American mechanical engineer Scott Cameron we finally laid the foundations of our habitat on the tall chairs of a

A design office is set up at the Under The Pole base in Concarneau, in the Explore Trust's premises. Scott, Ghislain, Sylvain, Emmanuelle and Gaël discuss the design of the Capsule.

café in Kodiak, Alaska. It would be rigid after all, consisting of an aluminium cylinder at the ends of which we would assemble two large hemispherical domes, with an open airlock underneath that would allow divers to enter and leave as they wished. It would be attached to two heavy ballasts that would anchor it to the bottom and give it the mobility that was so important for us. Both a survival shelter and an observatory, our habitat was taking shape. As a nod to the simultaneous conquests of space and the deep made during in the 1960s and 1970s, the source and inspiration for so many of my dreams, we would call it Capsule.

CONSTRUCTION

After a few more sketches, calculations, consideration of construction options and research in the appropriate literature, we specified a model. But everything still remained to be done: exact sizes, calculation of forces, choosing materials, printing out plans, construction. In short, we had our work cut out.

Having joined us for the winter of 2017–18, Scott was working on the design of the Capsule and its ballasts. At the same time Sylvain and I started work on the specifications of the peripheral systems, both for the Capsule's practical functions and for its system of atmospheric control and maintenance. How would we use it? What additional needs would we have? How would they impact the design?

This phase required a great amount of development, production and testing. To make the Capsule autonomous and independent of the surface, it would have to become a huge gas rebreather, similar to those we use when diving, but with one important difference: we would be inside it! Once immersed in the closed atmosphere of the capsule we would have to filter our CO_2 through a lime filter. The used oxygen would be reinjected automatically while maintaining a constant pressure of 0.4–0.5bar (5.8–7.25psi), using three oxygen sensors connected to a computer. All this partially redundant system could be overridden manually, and backed up by an independent system for the occupants to monitor the O_2, He, CO_2 and CO content of the atmosphere. For a time we considered entrusting this part of the project to an external subcontractor. After discussions with various French, Danish, Italian and Canadian manufacturers it appeared that there was no off-the-shelf system that suited our needs. The Capsule's size and volume meant that we had to develop its own system, taking certain constraints into account.

To ensure external control of the dives and provide permanent surveillance we equipped the Capsule with a video camera, microphone and headset, as well as a data transmission system to communicate with our base on land or on board the WHY. The Capsule would therefore be fully connected; we could even do videoconferencing, live from under the sea, via wifi! To enable this, a cable connected to an antenna floating above the Capsule would transmit its signals to one on land or at the top of the WHY's mast. Sitting in front of the monitors, the rest of the team

Above, top: A full-size model of the Capsule is built to test its habitability and test the placement of the different internal equipment.

Above: Sylvain works on the atmosphere control systems while Gaël finalizes the model in the sail loft.

Opposite, top and middle: The ballast tanks and the Capsule were built in the PIRIOU shipyards, next to our offices.

Opposite, bottom: At the end of June 2018, Ghislain, Sylvain and Erwan spend 24 hours inside the Capsule in the hangar, in the dry, to try out life on board and the correct functioning of the atmosphere control systems.

could watch and interact live with the divers. These two systems (atmospheric control and telecomms) were to be developed at our base in Concarneau, under the leadership of Sylvain Pujolle.

Capsule took shape little by little, as did its ballasts. Bit by bit our virtual Lego set was pieced together on our screens. In order to physically test out and confirm the consistency of our choices, we built a wooden scale model, to give ourselves a solid representation of the interior living space, test layout options and check whether all those products of our fevered imaginations would be feasible. By early spring 2018, Capsule's mechanical engineering was complete. After going out to tender locally, the PIRIOU shipyards in Concarneau were made responsible for construction. Within weeks, Capsule took shape amid the fire and sparks of cutting and soldering tools. From aluminium and steel sheets and tubes, Capsule and its ballasts were born, in the boilermaking workshops on the quayside.

I returned from Polynesia to Concarneau at the end of June 2018 to conduct a full-scale trial with three objectives: to test the pressure-resistance and tightness of the domes; test the atmosphere control and regulation system; and trying out life inside for three people for 24 hours.

    The weather is hot as the summer begins. We carry out the test on dry land, in a hangar at the Explore base where we have our offices. In the oven-like conditions of the Capsule, Sylvain Pujolle, Erwan Marivint and I are dripping with sweat. The temperature drops at night, making the experience much easier. The test is conclusive, we can now develop a working version of our system.

A few months later the ballasts, the Capsule and all the peripheral equipment are loaded into a 20ft container, which we will meet in Moorea, in French Polynesia, for a first mission from August to December 2019.

CAPSULE'S INNOVATIONS

SYLVAIN PUJOLLE
engineer and diver

Sylvain works on the system that controls and maintains the oxygen level in the Capsule's atmosphere.

Some of the questions that concerned me throughout the Capsule project and that I still think about every day of my working life as an engineer are: What is innovation? And what is its purpose?

Does it mean doing things that have never been done before? Or doing things that are already known about but doing them differently, because using a known process to achieve a different aim can also amount to innovation?

A large majority of divers know Jacques-Yves Cousteau's books and films; those of my generation even drew their inspiration from them. The most passionate have also followed the exploits of COMEX and other forerunners of all nationalities. Therefore even slightly knowledgeable divers know that undersea houses have already been built. Quite a few, in fact. To tell the truth, my biggest surprise when I started to study the Capsule project was to find out just how many habitats had been tried, and how daring the scientists and divers of the time had been.

"Man-in-the-Sea", "Precontinent I, II and III" (also called Conshelf), "SEALAB"[1], as well as German, Soviet, British and Romanian projects, had paved the way for deep-water, sustainable human habitats.

Leaning over my (virtual) drawing board, I was wondering how we could innovate when Cousteau, Fructus, Delauze, Stenuit, Link and many others had gone before us. These were daring men, with significant resources (offered by the oil industry, the US Navy, NASA or the Soviet army. As for the experiments they had conducted, they would never pass the scrutiny of an ethics committee today. Trying to innovate by always seeking to go "bigger", "deeper" or more "technical" would make no sense.

Seen from a different angle, innovation is an old story, a story of the constant consolidation and recycling of ideas. Plenty of ideas are not "new", many have already been tried and abandoned but may find relevance in another context.

Take electric cars for example – they were the first vehicles to exceed 100km an hour

(62.14mph, in 1899!) but then disappeared off the radar for more than a century before making a comeback in another context. Recyclers had been invented before scuba equipment, but were then set aside as being too dangerous, fit only for those divers often described as extremists or almost suicidal. In the 2000s, thanks to advances in electronics and the standardization of training, their technology became safe and accessible.

So was there any sense in rescuing from oblivion those undersea habitats that had been abandoned (or almost so) since the 1970s? Our answer was yes, but to use them for other objectives and to incorporate the most relevant technical advances.

For us, the first innovation in the Capsule was its objective, its *raison d'être*. Our predecessors had designed and operated their

1 "Man-in-the-Sea", Link and Stennuit; "Précontinent I, II & III" ("Conshelf"), Cousteau; "SEALAB", US Navy.

undersea homes like conquerors. It was the era of the "conquest of the deep" as well as the "conquest of space". The underwater village of Précontinent (Conshelf) was the site office and construction huts of future sea workers: miners, oil drillers and farmers. Levelling a reef to create a building site was not seen as an ethical problem: we were preparing to exploit the sea, so it made sense to level any obstacles we found there. I make no moral judgements here concerning the actions of the men of Cousteau's generation: they were of their time and they lived according to its values.

For our part, we thought of the Capsule as explorers would, not as conquerors. One of the challenges has been to design a system with a minimal, reversible footprint. Not disturbing the environment, observing silently, leaving without a trace, these were our essential stipulations, the *sine qua non* of our specifications. In practice, this led us to use a double ballast system, carefully proportioned, allowing installation, precise to a tiny fraction of an inch, close to the Capsule. Our habitat had to be able to ensure its occupants' rest and safety, without a support vessel above, or even nearby, to avoid the noise and impact of an anchorage.

We designed an autonomous air recirculation, gas monitoring and communication system that let us limit any extraneous equipment to a small surface buoy with a 2m (6ft 6in) pole. Two small batteries, the size of a 1lt ($1^3/_4$pt) flask, provided 24 hours of battery life. The miniaturization of electronic components has made possible for Capsule what was impossible 60 years ago, as everything (Capsule and its support material) had to fit inside a single 20-foot container, which in this mission would be shipped to Polynesia. A simple rigid inflatable boat was all that was needed to install the habitat almost 5 miles from its support base, which (apart from the team's kitchen) was limited to an antenna and a laptop. This

lightness and portability open up completely new possibilities for using a submarine habitat in remote or fragile sites.

Furthermore, part of our plan was that our innovation should be able to be shared, both economically and technically. Based on the principle that an extreme techno-futuristic feat, accessible only to a handful of exceptional people, had no place within the spirit of UTP, the innovations carried out for Capsule aimed to serve the scientific and ecological communities. In other words, groups of people for whom pure technical performance or unique achievements are not ends in themselves. Science must be able to replicate observations in order to be legitimized, and environmental preservation should be applicable to everyone. Thus we have chosen to develop the Capsule, not in a low-tech way, as such, but with technology that is straightforward and accessible. Wherever we could do without electronics and energy consumption we did so. Where electronics were essential (for atmospheric management and communications), we built them around open source[2] components and software.

The innovation here has thus been guided by the understatement that is so necessary in our times, as well as by its possible future exploitation by other teams of scientists. To my initial question, "What is the purpose of innovation today?" I therefore answer: to inspire, but principally to share the fruits of our thoughts and experiences with any reasonably well-organized and motivated team of researchers. ∎

_____
2 Raspberry Pi, Arduino, Debian...

Above top: Sylvain does a communication test with the ground base before the first 24-hour saturation in the Capsule.

Above: Sylvain and Ghislain discuss the tests to be carried out and how the launch should be organized. They have been friends for 25 years!

Site of Capsule

WHY's anchorage

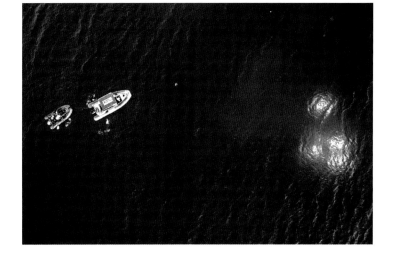

Opening the container housing the Capsule,
the ballast tanks and all its equipment.

Installing the antenna in the house's grounds.
It will let us communicate and exchange data with the Capsule.

SETTING UP

The Capsule programme begins with our team converging on Moorea in August 2019. The WHY is anchored in Opunohu Bay, near to CRIOBE, facing what will be our new headquarters: a large plot with a house and a pontoon giving direct access to the lagoon.

Opening the container in which Capsule, its ballasts and all the equipment have been shipped marks the start of the mission and a long period of preparatory work. While some of the team are busy assembling the domes and testing that the portholes are watertight, others use a thruster to survey the reef and identify the best sites for the installation. Meals prepared by the kitchen team lend a rhythm to the days. The dive team is organized around dozens of oxygen and helium B50s[1], assembling cylinders, valves and regulators, and preparing the RIB (rigid inflatable boat) while the inflation station is running from morning till night. In short, Opunohu Bay is a real hive of activity.

On 22nd August we install the ballasts at sea, having previously trained on the sandy bottom of the lagoon. Each weighing 3 tonnes (3.3 tons), they are towed on the surface before being lined up with the selected site. Gradually filled with water, they sink slowly until they weigh only a few pounds. Yard by yard, foot by

foot, Sylvain and I control them as they descend from the huge floats suspending them from the surface, while Emmanuelle, Erwan, Julien and Nico guide them into place with the help of their scooters. Around us, Aldo, Franck and Victor take pictures. I am amazed at the ease and precision, to a fraction of an inch, with which we manoeuvre them to drop into place side by side on the seabed of sand and dead coral. At 23m down (76ft), opposite a magnificent coral pinnacle, we moor them one to the other, opening wide all the valves to release the remaining volume of air. With each litre (61 in³) expelled, an extra kilo (2.2lb) of ballast will anchor the Capsule. In a few minutes the operation is complete and the Capsule's seabed moorings are ready. Each successful step is a relief because, although we have tried to think of everything, uncertainties remain.

On 17th September all systems are go. It's so unusual that I can scarcely believe it! We have just received the final administrative authorisation, triggering Capsule's launch. From the moment the announcement is made the pace quickens: along a few miles of road, shaded by coconut palms, we reach the small port of Papetoaï, where Capsule is delicately placed across our 4.2m (14ft) rigid inflatable boat under the curious, amused gaze of the local children. The sight is so surprising because of its contrast with the disproportionate resources usually used to support life beneath the sea. I like Capsule's simplicity because it confirms the

1 Fifty-litre (1.76ft³) bottles of oxygen or helium.

Emmanuelle seems a little doubtful
about the Capsule's living space.

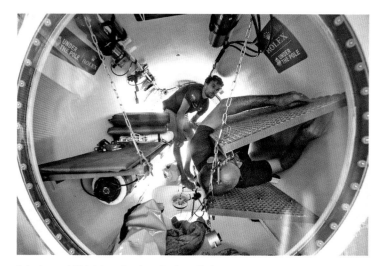

Sylvain and Ghislain adjusting the installation
and testing the Capsule's interior equipment.

basic idea of the project, which is meant to be as unfussy as possible. All in all, it only needed a flatbed truck from the island's DIY store to take the Capsule and its ballasts out of their 20ft container and put them into the water. A few straps, a 20-horsepower outboard motor and we reach the WHY's anchorage across the lagoon, where she will spend her last night on the surface. A few hours later, sitting at the table with the rest of the team, I savour this moment, looking out at the WHY with the Capsule seeming to smile at me in the setting sun. It reminds me of our time at the Eureka station in the far north of Canada in March 2010, when the team and I were enjoying our last warm evening together before being dropped off at the North Pole the next day. There is still much to be done, but as those who have led an expedition know, when you start off under the right conditions, it is because you have already come a long way and faced many pitfalls. Everything is ready and at the evening briefing we are divided into teams.

The next day, just as forecast, the weather is fine and, most importantly, the sea is calm. Sailing to the site, slightly less than 2 miles away, gives us time to enjoy this moment, which I share with Sylvain. On the WHY, which is escorting us, the divers get ready. Once we are lined up with the ballasts, which are clearly visible from the surface, everyone gets into position. We detach the Capsule and with a strong push it rolls, then tilts. Amid all the joy and excitement we have to stay alert to avoid injuring ourselves or damaging its large windows. At first it fills slowly, then suddenly sinks, coming under tension beneath the buoys that mark

its position on the surface. It is a similar manoeuvre to the one we carried out with the ballasts, so we are confident. We lower it gradually as the underwater scooters tow it towards its landing zone. We moor its four suspended guy ropes to their respective mooring points. With relative ease, in a slow continuous movement, Capsule moves into place. Emmanuelle approaches the airlock and slips in a regulator which flushes out the water from inside via the airlock, just enough to put it under slight tension and adjust its trim and depth. We release the floats, which spin towards the surface like rockets. For the first time, Capsule appears just as we had imagined and designed her. As soon as Emmanuelle has finished filling her, I remove my rebreather, hang it up outside, and hold my breath as I glide towards the "moon pool"[2]. I emerge within, climb the ladder, sit inside the capsule and scream with delight as I watch my comrades rush to join me one by one. We hug, check each other over, kiss and congratulate each other. It is an underwater explosion of joy for us as we experience for the first time the ultimate feeling of living under the sea.

A major programme now awaits, in preparation for the first 24-hour dive, which will begin two days later. For us to be able to stay in the Capsule for long periods it first has to be completely purged of air by refilling it with water, then filling it with a ready-made mixture of 14% oxygen and 86% helium. Then we must install the system that filters, maintains and controls its new atmosphere, as well as the telecomms system that allows radio communication with our base, enables live video links and transmits all the control parameters for safety purposes. Sylvain has supervised the sequence of lowering all the equipment, which arrives one piece at a time in shuttles. These pressurized containers are used to ferry sensitive equipment, new filters, meals and dry clothes up and down between the surface and the Capsule. The atmosphere is not fully saturated yet, so time is running out!

Sylvain and I have known each other for 25 years. Meeting him was one of the encounters that have shaped my life. A unique personality, he taught me to dive when I started at the Glénan International Diving Centre, but above all he taught me and the other young instructors not to be satisfied with the bare minimum but to explore subjects in depth and always have a questioning viewpoint. An incredibly versatile and talented engineer,

2   The Capsule's entrance and exit airlock.

Tommy, Clément, Yann, Sylvain, Erwan and Ghislain
finish fixing the domes. Next, they will fill the Capsule
with water to test its watertightness.

Loading the Capsule. *Right:* Launching from the crane truck directly onto the RIB, watched by curious children. *Top:* Launching the Capsule on its site.

as good with mechanics as computer science, electronics or communication systems, he is also an excellent technician. A real builder! Although I sometimes tear my hair out when faced with his organisation and seemingly casual attitude towards the ideas that I am trying to achieve, I can also see in it a kind of rejection of conformity to the established order, constantly forcing us to question ourselves. Appropriately applied, this helps to raise the standard of our projects. Sylvain is a free spirit, unmanageable, endearing and brilliant. Even more important is the sincere, deep friendship that he has brought Manue and me, an unparalleled loyalty and deep mutual respect. I know that I can count on him at all times, which makes him an invaluable teammate.

On board Capsule, the service divers send Sylvain and me the first shuttles: lime filters, odour filters, fans, oxygen sensors, control box, telecomms box, batteries, cabling of all kinds... the Capsule comes to life. With the last connections made, we start testing the connection with Tommy, who, 2.5km away ($1^1/_2$ miles) as the crow flies, has just seen us appear on his screen: "Hello capsule, I can see you and hear you. Can you hear me? O_2: 14% and 0.4bar (5.8psi), He: 86%, CO_2: 0%, CO: 0%... It all looks good here". That's it then, Capsule is breathing and she is just waiting for us all to arrive.

The ballast tanks are set down here with great precision on a sea bed of sand and dead coral.

An abseil system is installed with buoys on the surface to control the descent. The divers guide the Capsule, towing it to its site with their thrusters to attach it to the ballast tanks.

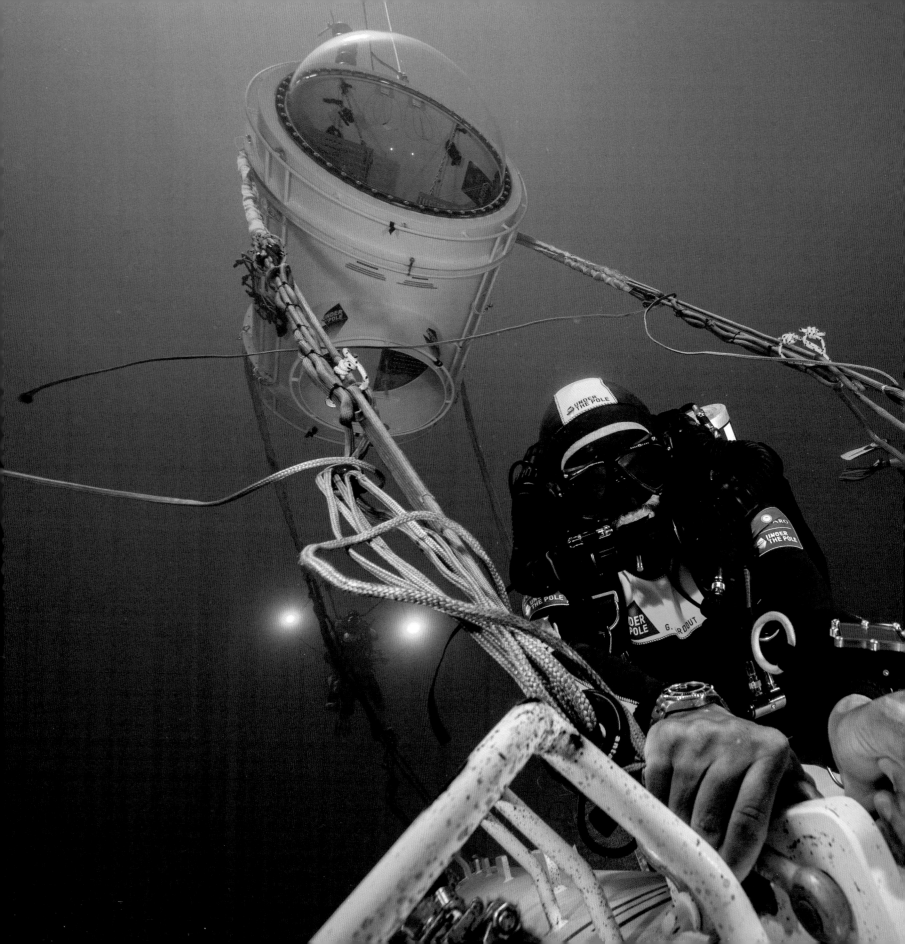

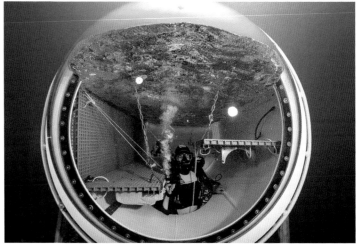

Left: Within minutes, the four slings are attached to the ballast tanks. Under low tension, their adjustment allows the Capsule's depth and trim to be adjusted.

Above top: Emmanuelle blows air into the Capsule to expel the water inside.

Above: First moments inside the Capsule – Ghislain smiles as his dream comes true!

DECOMPRESSION,
OR HOW TO RETURN TO THE SURFACE FROM THE CAPSULE

BERNARD GARDETTE
D.Sc, former scientific director of COMEX

Professional divers practise saturation diving in order to be able to work underwater for a long time without having to ascend after each dive. The time needed to return to the surface is the same however long has been spent under pressure; it depends only on the depth. As it is difficult to stay underwater for more than a few hours while diving, it is necessary to use either an underwater habitat, such as Cousteau's house under the sea, or a turret-caisson assembly, as practised by COMEX since the 1960s. The divers live under pressure in caissons (compression chambers) on board a boat on the surface and descend to work at the bottom using the diving turret. For practical and safety reasons, underwater habitats are usually only positioned at shallow depths. For the Capsule mission, a site was chosen at a depth of 20m (66ft), to suit the needs of the scientific observation programme, close to a drop-off that allows deeper excursions. It is also a good compromise between a relatively short distance and time to the surface in case of emergency evacuation and a sufficient depth to give shelter from the swell. Heliox (a mixture of helium and oxygen) was soon established as the gas of choice for Capsule as it provides a faster, safer

decompression than nitrogen in air. A long period of fine-tuning the procedure was required, however, as this type of shallow saturation is not widely practiced in professional diving. Stopovers in the habitat are therefore carried out under Heliox at 20m (66ft), with an oxygen pressure of 0.4 bar, and an ascent to the surface in four hours under 1.3 bar. To avoid the divers being immersed for too long during decompression, they stay in the dry, inside Capsule, breathing for two hours on their diving rebreathers, then take a further two hours to return to the surface, stopping for 25 minutes every 3m (10ft) from 15m (50ft) while in the water. Leaving Capsule at 20m (66ft), trips down to between 15m and 35m (50–115ft) are made for unlimited times without decompression stops before returning to the habitat. This procedure of saturation diving with sorties outside the habitat allows much longer dives than starting from the surface. Given the small volume of Capsule (4.3m3/152 cu.ft.), we limited the number of people inside to two or three for three days at a time. The environmental parameters are well controlled: good oxygen regulation, good carbon dioxide elimination and a comfortable temperature of 30°C. Teams of divers worked

continuously in the Capsule for more than two months. No incident or accident occurred, so the procedures have ensured a good standard of safety throughout the mission. Furthermore, the results of the physiological measurements show that saturation diving under Capsule conditions is less aggressive to the body than normal scuba diving. It is therefore possible to adapt Heliox saturation diving to light, easily set up, inexpensive underwater habitats with the same safety as in professional diving. Capsule is now an indispensable tool for observing the behaviour of underwater wildlife in the mesophotic zone, which is still little studied, and this can be done without any impact on the environment. In the near future, we can imagine several Capsules positioned at different depths to allow scientific missions down to 100m (330ft).

Ghislain and Gaël complete half of their decompression in the dry, using their rebreathers, before leaving to complete their decompression stages. In total, after a saturation stay in Capsule, it takes just over 4 hours to return to the surface.

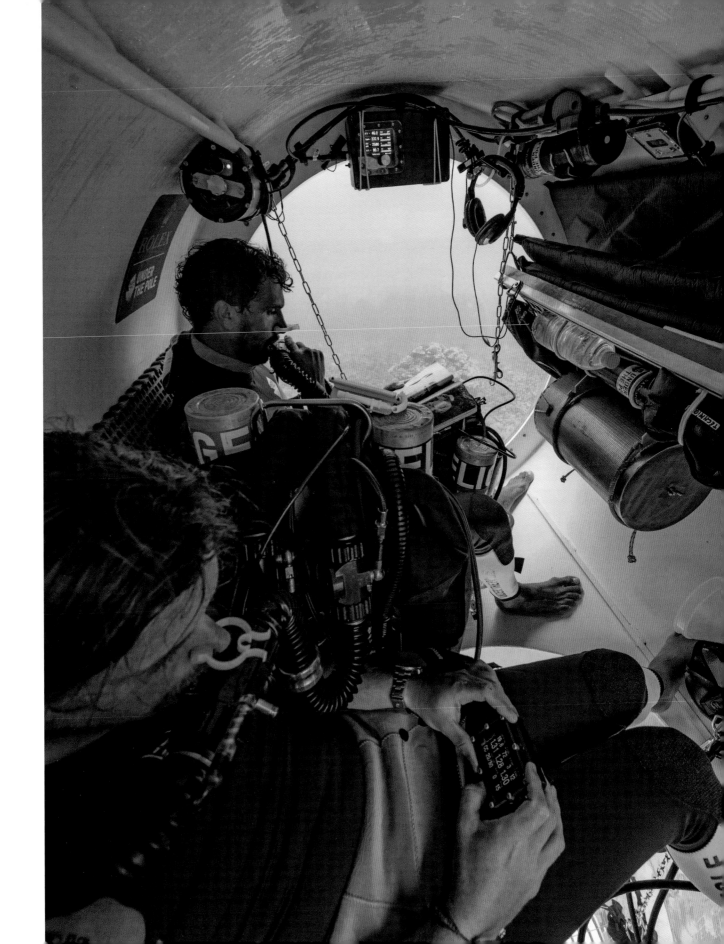

THE FIRST 24HRS
IN THE CAPSULE

20th September 2019

On the surface, I breathe into my rebreather and with a final wave of my hand I salute the team who are smiling at me from the RIB. Beneath my flippers, 20m down (66ft), the Capsule awaits me. Today I am submerging myself and not expecting to re-emerge! This fundamentally unnatural idea contradicts a diver's training, which, from their first immersion, aims to teach them to always return to the surface safely. A strange feeling, an antagonistic uneasiness, grips me. Part of me (my brain), rationalizes the situation, reminding me that "everything is under control, everything has been tested and is working perfectly". Another part of me, the physical, instinctive one, seems to slow my descent, as if to remind me that there is nothing natural in what I am about to do: "living under the sea is something fishy!" This is the first time that I have felt such a feeling, simultaneously so strong and irresistibly exciting: I am going to live under the sea!

With a few strokes of my flippers I approach the Capsule. It is beautiful, serene in the apparent calm of the reef. Everything is ready and has been carefully prepared in the previous hours: the bottles of oxygen and heliox (oxygen/ helium) supplying the Capsule's atmosphere; carefully stored heliox bottles with their regulators that will allow divers to exit and enter freely; head lights and their batteries; one waterproof bag for each team member; evacuation kits and the emergency decompression line placed a short distance away from the ballasts. This line is our rescue parachute. To reassure ourselves we have planned and practised the worst evacuation scenarios. They all begin: "In the dead of night, in complete darkness..." to which are added various more or less rational possibilities: (scenario of the anchors failing) "a shock, like a rupture... water rushes violently into our Capsule, which has tipped over..." or else: (scenario of one of our Li-ion batteries catching fire) "...a cry of alarm, we are suffocating, our eyes sting..." In all cases the procedure to follow is identical: "Grab my mask, my micro-bottle and my emergency lamp, exit through the airlock, help my friends... find the emergency decompression line by grabbing hold of the ballasts..." The procedure is a simple one: if the team on watch above loses contact or witnesses an evacuation being carried out they will trigger the alarm and within 15 minutes three divers will arrive with lights and wetsuits, soon we will have sandwiches and coffee (to comfort us, like children's "blankies")... These are the best procedures we can devise to reassure ourselves!

Sylvain and Victor, our cameraman, are accompanying me for this first 24-hour stay in the Capsule. Arriving on the platform

Jacques-Yves Cousteau said, "The best way to observe a fish is to become a fish." In the Capsule, the wildlife forgets about us and the domes are perfect for discreet observation.

Life on board Capsule is spartan. We often sleep fitfully, each with a mask, lamp and small bottle available, in case we have to evacuate in an emergency during the night.

underneath the airlock I open my diving suit, take out my mouthpiece, gently extricate myself from the rebreather and hang it underneath the Capsule, then finally enter the airlock. Sylvain is ahead of me and checks that the installation is working correctly. The atmosphere is absolutely calm, as if life here is governed by different codes. I hear the crackling of the reef and the hum of the fan as it forces our breathing mixture of gases through the fan. Through the two giant portholes I can see the fish coming and going on the reef, oblivious to our presence. The humidity is high in here and a thin layer of condensation settles on the domes, which we regularly wipe down with a sponge. As if to fully establish my new position as a human being living under the sea I take off my wetsuit and put on shorts and a T-shirt.

It's not time to relax yet. Victor has joined us and we must take delivery of the shuttles containing our meals and the camera. It's time to put everything neatly away; our companions are already heading back to the surface, having inspected the outside of the Capsule. A last wave of the hand, smiles… Finally we are alone… Now our experience of life under the sea can really begin.

The objective of these first 24 hours is to make sure that the atmospheric maintenance and telecomms systems are working properly, to see how we feel in ourselves, to see how best to organize life on board as well as assistance and surveillance from the surface. Above all else, though, it is to provide as many answers as possible to the many questions that we have been asking ourselves over the past three years: will we suffer from the cold in our helium-charged atmosphere? Will the condensation affect our comfort and will it be a problem for the on-board electronics? How reliable and durable will the technologies that support us prove to be? Will our own bodily odours make the Capsule impossible to breathe in or will the carbon filter work successfully?

And the first good news is that we aren't cold! We had considered wearing heated fleece clothing, but in the end, with this 26°C (78.8°F) water surrounding us and in spite of the 86% helium that we are breathing, we can wear light clothing just as we would on the surface!

What a vision! Beneath me extends something resembling a city with its inhabitants who run around and interact. I do not yet understand all their codes and behaviours, but we can clearly see that the reef in front of our eyes teems with structured activity, governed by invisible rules. As each minute spent here saturates my body with more helium, lengthening the decompression stages that I will need before I can return to the surface, I experience a curious sensation. For the first time in my diving career, I have time!

With the setting of the sun the mood changes. The light fades quickly and the reef gradually disappears into deep shade, then total darkness. Alone in our "capsule" of life, we seem totally isolated. Our meal marks a comforting, convivial moment in the day. Fully prepared in advance, it reminds me of our expedition rations at the Pole.

Like all "first times", my first night in the Capsule is filled with curiosity, uncertainty, mystery, recklessness and a little bit of worry. Lying in our bunks like sardines in a tin, we observe the sleeping reef through the portholes. We discuss our impressions and offer our respective "sea camper tips" for making our refuge more comfortable. Slowly our eyes grow tired and at last we nod off, though we don't sleep soundly. I regularly note the figures and graphs on the screens out of the corner of my eye. I hear my companions shifting their positions, a sign that, like me, they are trying to get to sleep. In the middle of the night we hear a sound: a humpback whale is singing somewhere in the ocean. For over an hour we listen to him come closer. How magical! The singing male draws near to us… How far away? We can't tell. Perhaps he will soar over us without being seen. But the strength of his song leaves no doubt about how close he is. We even feel his vibrations resonating on the aluminium envelope separating us from the sea. He leaves in the same way that he had arrived, without lingering over us, continuing his mysterious nocturnal journey along the reef. Overwhelmed by tiredness, we finally sink into sleep.

In the early hours I suddenly awaken from a strange dream, in which a whale calf is rubbing itself against the capsule and dragging it to the bottom. Scolded by its mother, it flounced off, and I realise that, mistaking the white Capsule for his mother's belly, it had snuggled up against us just as it would have done against her![4] In a few minutes, life resumes its normal course around us. Parrotfish roam the reef, surgeonfish pick busily at the seaweed attached to the rock, schools of humpback red snappers swim around the domes. We extricate ourselves from our beds as if we were emerging numbly from our sleeping bags after a tormented night in a tent in the mountains. We fold and tidy away our bedding and in a few minutes we are again sitting side by side, eating a hearty breakfast. The watchers on the surface call us, having followed our every move on their control screens throughout the night.

At the beginning of the afternoon, after putting on our wetsuits, which have been flattened by 24 hours under pressure, we slip one by one into the airlock to start our decompression. In the water, the other divers have returned and they share knowing looks with us. With flippers on and recyclers on our backs, we begin a slow ascent that will last five hours.[5] With the sun sinking towards the horizon once more, we lift our heads above water after 27hrs 20 minutes in the ocean. Despite the tiredness, the whole team is celebrating: "We have slept under the sea!"

Above, top: Departures and returns from Capsule are always high points, when team members come to encourage and ask questions... Here, Sylvain and Victor emerge from the first 24 hours underwater and give their impressions to Bernard.

Above: Tom says goodbye to Ghislain who is leaving for his first night underwater.

1   Divers who stay in the capsule during saturation report having had particularly strange, original dreams. Is it a product of the out-of-the ordinary experience? The helium that we breathe? No study ever seems to have been done into the subject, but it seems that the sleeping conditions on board the Capsule impact on our nocturnal thoughts. A subject for future study!

2   The decompression procedure will be reduced to four hours thereafter, two of which will be done inside the Capsule, using rebreathers.

STUDYING THE PHYSIOLOGY OF DIVERS ON VERY DEEP OR PROLONGED DIVES

[1]ORPHY (Laboratory for the Optimization of Physiological Regulations), University of Western Brittany, Brest

[2]TEK diving SAS

[3]Hyperbaric medicine and diving skills service, Sainte-Anne HIA (Army Training Hospital), Toulon

The divers are subjected to a battery of tests by doctors and physiology researchers before each departure and immediately upon their return.

Expeditions such as those of Under The Pole III subject divers, both male and female, to extreme living conditions never experienced before. Whether it is repeated autonomous deep dives (below 100m [330ft] in depth) for several months, during DeepHope, or staying in shallow saturation (where the diver is permanently under pressure) in the Capsule underwater observatory (five times smaller than the cockpits used for professional diving in "classic" saturation), almost nothing is known about the ability of humans to withstand such stresses.

How well can repeated high pressure scuba dives be tolerated? How well do the divers, individually and as a group, cope with being confined, remaining under low pressure for several days while breathing exotic mixtures of gases? Can we consider extending these diving programmes by identifying and preventing physiological risks?

By their exceptional nature, these expeditions offer physiologists an ideal opportunity to study, in real conditions, the capacity of human beings to adapt to the conditions of extreme diving, whether in terms of depth or duration.

Thus, to give marine biologists a light, self-sufficient , transportable tool allowing them to observe the underwater environment 24 hours a day, the Capsule programme has developed the concept of a "bungalow under the sea": an easily movable habitat requiring only minimal logistics and in which two or even three divers can stay for several days. The technological solutions that have made this possible necessitate significant confinement ($4.3m^3$ [$152ft^3$] for three divers, with almost no possibility of standing upright) in potentially challenging conditions (humidity, heat and ventilation with a breathing mixture based on helium, hyperoxia –excessive oxygen or oxygen pressure). This cocktail has never been encountered before, either in previous experiments with undersea houses or in industrial saturation diving. One of the main challenges was to devise, thanks to the multidisciplinary work of physiologists and doctors, an accelerated decompression procedure to allow a rapid return to the surface in a few hours, despite having stayed under pressure for several days. This was possible thanks to a thorough analysis of the risk-benefit balance with respect to the level of hyperoxia and the final duration of decompression.

The hyperoxia and decompression tolerance criteria have thus been crucial parameters in designing a safe decompression procedure. Beyond these issues, it seemed to us essential to study the cardiocirculatory and neuropsychological changes that confinement in the Capsule would impose by limiting the living space and physical activity of the subjects. Therefore the physiological measurements taken included the recording and analysis of the electrocardiogram, pulmonary parameters and oxygen saturation, as well as the daily evaluation of fatigue (flicker fusion threshold) and mood (PANAS questionnaire[1]) during the stay in the Capsule and up to 24 hours after leaving. The quality of decompression was also assessed. All these measurements indicated good tolerance by all the divers, which made it possible not only to confirm Capsule's viability, but also to give the go-ahead for the other marine biologists to stay there during the rest of the programme. Beyond the strict domain of diving, the knowledge gained by this study will also be relevant to other situations involving confinement and physical inactivity (in submarines, space exploration and so on).

On the other hand, even though closed-circuit rebreather exploratory dives beyond 100m (330ft) are uncommon, they are nonetheless also being done – and ever more frequently – by other divers (scientists, cavers or recreational divers). However, the "deepest" physiological measurements had been taken after dives at 85m (276ft) breathing trimix or heliox in a conventional diving suit. Therefore, prior to those obtained during DeepHope, no data existed on the effects of this type of exploratory dive and even less on repeating them. This expedition made it possible to study for the first time a series of trimix dives between 90 and 120m deep (295–394ft). Measurements carried out on the UTP III divers showed a significant decrease in lung capacity (of the order of 30% after a single dive) and incomplete

recovery 24 hours after leaving the water. They also showed a water loss of around 3kg (6lb 10 oz) on average. These changes are much greater than what had previously been observed for dives below 100m (330ft); if confirmed by future studies, UTP III data will have contributed to improving risk prevention through better knowledge of the constraints that deep rebreather diving imposes. They will also be useful for updating the criteria to be taken into account when organising dives and/or for assessing the medical suitability of divers (professional and recreational), for this sort of diving.

Thus, the study of physiological responses under these unusual circumstances has two interests.

In the short term (that is, during the expedition) it allows the "physiological monitoring" of the divers to ensure the proper functioning (homeostasis, as we call it) of the major functions (cardiovascular, respiratory etc.), thus providing the doctor with data additional to his own observations so as to enable him to detect any health problem at an early stage.

In the medium and long term, by their non-standard nature, these diving exploration programmes represent opportunities to better understand the human capacity to adapt to diving, by identifying physiological modifications to repeated autonomous deep dives on the one hand and, on the other, how individuals and groups respond to saturation diving experiences in confined spaces. ∎

1   This scale of positive and negative feelings is a questionnaire designed to measure mood and emotions.

Julien tests for the presence of bubbles circulating in Erwan's bloodstream after a deep dive.

HELLO SEA, THIS IS EARTH SPEAKING

Apolline prepares the aquanauts' rations.

Team work! This is what you sense above all when you stand back to look down at the buzzing hive that our playground around our HQ has become, from the CRIOBE to the Capsule. On the surface our pace of life is dictated by our meals, and by the time on board the Capsule. And she, as is customary in the Tropics, is governed by the rhythm of the sun. The day begins with breakfast, followed by a 7am briefing, after Robin and Tom have gone off to school in Moorea. We take stock of the programme, the teams, the team leaders and the important events. Then begins the waltz of cars and bicycles as we leave for "office work" at CRIOBE, or to refill bottles, carry out refuelling or collect equipment from the container. The diving team prepares the rebreathers, repacks a filter for the Capsule or puts meals prepared by the kitchen into the shuttle. We have lunch, take stock of the programme once more and start again.

Briefings usually bring a smile to the face, because they too are a routine that helps to break up the day. They are essential and as short as possible while lasting as long as is necessary. And everyone must listen attentively, because they are the key to a successful, efficient operation. Objectives, timing, teams, managers, points of vigilance, information to be taken into account, safety reminders or changes of protocol… everything that must be heard has been said. Any questions? Have a good day!

The teams rotate. A diver may have an earache, so they rest, becoming a pilot or an inflator. Is a helping hand needed with machinery on board the WHY, or are four volunteers needed to meet and greet a school party? We work it out, swap roles, give a little of our spare time. Mutual assistance and benevolence are essential. There are several ways to run a programme like Capsule, which inevitably demands a lot of work, thoroughness and commitment. There are many ways to experience it and remember it. As we see it, one of the most important things is the state of mind in which everyone tackles their mission. It translates on a daily basis into an attitude that will make a group coalesce or not, that will give a team wings or prevent it from ever taking off. To be of service, to respect everyone, to trust, to laugh and to be self-deprecating, this state of mind is a skill that has to be learnt and practised. It is fundamental to major projects.

Every day we stick up, or tear down, sheets of paper in the bay window of the house overlooking the WHY at anchor in the lagoon: rotas for diving, pilots, rest periods, inflators, as well as a checklist and calendar to remind everyone of the day's programme. Next to it, in a converted office corner that we sometimes call "Houston" is our "mission control", that makes it possible to observe, 24 hours a day, by way of a monitor, everything that is being said, happening and being done in the Capsule. We all do two-hour shifts in front of the screens, passing information to the onboard crew or listening to them.

Once the day's work is done, everyone gathers in the house. A few minutes of packing things away and sweeping up and then it's time for a drink. This tradition has come from life on board the WHY and it allows everyone to unwind informally with a cold beer, to relax, laugh and debrief as required. Meanwhile, down on the dark reef, 20m (66ft) below the surface, the Capsule's "aquanauts" settle down to dine.

Briefings are held every day to make sure that the programme runs smoothly. Usually short, they sometimes need more time, as seen here, before the departure for the first saturation dive.

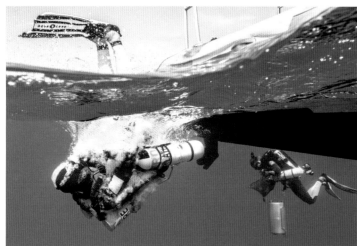

Above, top: Nico prepares the different gas mixes in our inflation station at CRIOBE.

Above: The support divers plunge in, with shuttles to supply the aquanauts. Once their cargo is deposited, they will do a general inspection of the Capsule and brush it clean.

Right: From the drone, the Capsule is clearly visible on the sea floor at 23m (75ft). Its surface buoy's antenna allows communication with the base on land.

Robin and Tom call Emmanuelle before going to sleep and ask about the Capsule experiment. Her helium-modified voice does not worry them and the boys tell her about their day at school.

THREE DAYS
BENEATH THE SEA

An extract from Emmanuelle Périé-Bardout's logbook

As I submerge myself to begin three days under the sea, my last scraps of apprehension disappear. How stage fright disappears when it is time to go onstage.

Despite my reluctance, I always knew in my heart that I would be taking this trip. How can I be afraid when I'm about to make a childhood dream come true? I can remember myself at Robin's age, engrossed in Cousteau's documentaries, books and comics. They filled my whole life and from my 6th floor apartment in Troyes en Champagne, I wondered how I could fulfil my dreams. Now, at the dawn of having this extraordinary experience, my excitement grows, as if I were rediscovering those childish feelings.

I didn't sleep well the night before leaving for the Capsule. It reminded me of another night, the day before the DC3 dropped us off onto the pack ice at the North Pole. In the darkness of my room, I imagined myself in the darkness of the ocean and whispered that I was apprehensive. Ghislain replied, with his usual composure, "You're going to love it". Good.

Now I watch the impressive mountains of Opunohu Bay disappear and turn towards Capsule, which appears in the blue. Even when I step inside, I still find it hard to believe that I will be living here for three days. Ghislain has come to say goodbye to me from outside the dome. He shakes his head at my emotional reaction and the smile in his eyes is priceless. I've loved this boy for almost 15 years and our relationship works so well because we understand each other. My happiness chimes with him because he has known it himself.

How can I describe life at a depth of 20m (66ft)? In our cocoon we are gently rocked by the swell and our ears are continually compensating for it. The colours are different, smells are heightened, and of course our voices are transformed by the helium (Donald Duck would seem almost sexy next to us).
Three days, it's both a long time and a short one...

Some days were magical but there was one really tough one. On the second day I woke up with a headache and nausea that eventually forced me to return from my diving excursion. I paid dearly

The oxygen injection system has developed a fault.
Emmanuelle, in saturation with Victor and Julien,
talks to the surface. Outside, the safety divers are
arriving to solve the problem.

for my reluctance to hydrate myself before the first night, which, added to the discomfort of the plastic bunk, had triggered this headache. Our doctor, Emmanuel Goin, brought me an appropriate treatment and I recovered easily.

The sunsets and sunrises on the reef that we were observing for the scientific programme quickly became absorbing to watch. Being able to sit in the dry and watch, without a time limit, underwater life proceed according to the time of day has been thrilling. I learned more about fish in three days than in 15 years of scuba diving. There had been that first night, the one that I dreaded, yet as soon as darkness had fallen, the magic began to happen. We exclaimed at the mesmerising spectacle of zooplankton, tiny jellyfish and huge phosphorescent worms as they rippled past the thin stream of light from our lamps, and our two trumpetfish (soon named Miles and Louis[1]) who were launching lightning attacks before returning to their lookout points. On the seabed, a silvertip shark slipped between the mounds of coral. Suddenly, whalesong invaded our small habitat until it vibrated. That first night I fell asleep after reading a few pages of Philip Pullman's *La Belle Sauvage*[2] while thinking that I myself was at a crossroads between two worlds. I had strange, beautiful, scary, powerful dreams before we awoke.

Victor, Julien and I shared countless fits of laughter, especially when we had to pee in a tube for the physio programme – something that was already complicated enough, particularly for me. Another memorable occasion was when the surface forgot to send down forks on the night we were having spaghetti.

Impressions: moments alone in the capsule when it felt like being in *Abyss* or *Gravity*. How emotional I felt when I received a drawing from Tom showing the sun (when I had seen neither one for two days). That diced blue ham[3] that we didn't want to eat any more, and the chocolate bar that was gobbled up. The permanent humidity. Moisture that never left our skin. Going to the bathroom – I'll spare you the details but in summary, peeing into the moon pool (and collecting that famous daily sample) but going outside to do the rest – without being surprised by passing divers. Having no choice about being self-deprecating because it's always better to laugh about it. There was Bernard's snorkelling visit, calls from Robin and Tom asking whether I'd had a good day in the capsule and arguing who should speak to me first. There was the oxygen injector failure on the last evening and the fear (fortunately soon ruled out) that we would have to evacuate the Capsule in the dark. There was the last day, when I woke at 4am and couldn't get to sleep again because the whales' singing was so close by. The full moon was reflected on the surface. I stood and watched life awakening and let melancholy flood through me as I thought of the IPCC report predicting that all corals will be wiped out by 2050. Robin will be 38 and Tom 34.

Finally there was the departure. Decompression. Two hours spent breathing with our rebreathers in the capsule in the most uncomfortable position imaginable, jaw cramps and a trickle of drool under the mouthpiece, the height of gracefulness (any comparison with *Gravity* forgotten). But they had brought us some music and I think we must have looked really crazy trying to dance in that position! The last two hours of ascending 3m (10ft) every 25 minutes, gripped by cold in our wetsuits that had been crushed by the constant pressure, were long ones. Robin's surprise visit to say "Hi!" at 6m (20ft) made the final stages pass more quickly. After 77 hours we returned to the surface.

How can I describe the contradictory emotions that I felt on getting out of the water? Rediscovering colours, my own voice, Robin and Tom's smiles, Ghislain's pride and, quite simply, the air. I feel quite literally as if I'm floating on the ground. I still have a lot of difficulty putting this experience into words because it was so unique. It's like beholding something in a dream. But I know already that this will always remain one of my most beautiful journeys.

---

1   In reference to Miles Davies and Louis Armstrong, nicknames that seemed appropriate for trumpet fish.

2   Philip Pullman is an English author best known for the trilogy His Dark Materials (called *À la croisée des mondes* – "At the crossroads between worlds" – in French).

3   Red or pink are seen as blue or green underwater.

Saturation divers leave the Capsule each day
to continue counting fish by species within the
two study areas near the Capsule.

Ghislain observes the life of the reef from the dome while a team
swims past outside. At night, the dynamics change and the species
and behaviours observed are different from those seen during the day.

A turtle, resident on the Capsule site,
is about to come up to the surface to breathe.

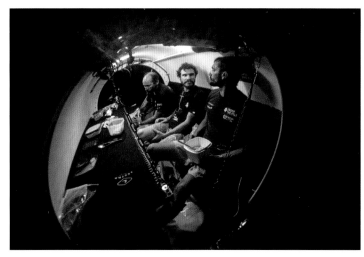

Above, top and bottom: Refuelling, meals, resting, diving
and watching fish set the pace of life in the Capsule.

Right: The whole set-up: Capsule and its ballast tanks,
the safety line marked by yellow parachutes, the cable at
the end of which are the buoy and the surface antenna
allowing communications with the outside world.

THE AQUANAUTS

The divers with their kit before entering the capsule:

19th–20th September 2019 (24hrs)
Ghislain Bardout, Sylvain Pujolle, Victor Rault

25th–28th September 2019 (72hrs)
Ghislain Bardout, Franck Gazzola, Gaël Lagarrigue

2nd–5th October 2019 (72hrs)
Aldo Ferrucci, Erwan Marivint, Sylvain Pujolle

9th–12th October 2019 (72hrs)
Emmanuelle Périé-Bardout, Julien Leblond,
Victor Rault

16th–19th October 2019 (72hrs)
Ghislain Bardout, Gaël Lagarrigue

19th–22nd October 2019 (72hrs)
Aldo Ferrucci, Erwan Marivint

22nd–25th October 2019 (72hrs)
Clément Madelaine, Nicolas Mollon

25th–28th October 2019 (72hrs)
Nicolas Paulme, Sylvain Pujolle

1st–2nd November 2019 (24hrs)
Gaël Lagarrigue, Gil Siu

2nd–3rd November 2019 (24hrs)
Ghislain Bardout, Victor Rault, Gil Siu

11th–12th November 2019 (24hrs)
Ghislain Bardout, Sylvain Pujolle, Victor Rault

14th–15th November 2019 (24hrs)
Daniel Cron, Julien Leblond, Yann Poupart

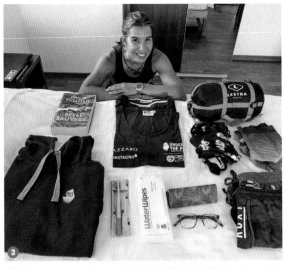

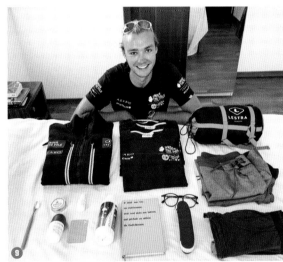

CORAL SPAWNING

BY FRANCK GAZZOLA

When Ghislain and Emmanuelle were discussing the scientific applications of the Capsule with CRIOBE, Laëtitia Hédouin proposed documenting, for the first time, corals spawning on the Polynesian outer reef. The idea was simple: to document the spawning of *Acropora hyacinthus*, which is said to take place in the early part of the night within a 9-day period following the full moon. This would, therefore, require long dives, at night, repeated over an unpredictable number of days. So the Capsule seemed like the ideal tool, provided you can find corals that are ready to spawn nearby. Yes, but…

The reconnaissance work with Yan Lacube from CRIOBE involves diving to identify colonies on the verge of spawning. Laëtitia Hédouin had told me beforehand how to spot the little pink eggs. But after surveying the entire area surrounding the capsule, all of the hyacinthus colonies are either dead, covered in green algae, or showing no signs of nearing reproduction. It seems that the recent bleaching episode has affected this species.

A new dive is arranged, with Laëtitia to help me and to enlarge to search area. Despite her expertise, the results are the same: out of 217 colonies, only nine survive: the loss is terrible. As she explains to me, in times of great stress, corals focus their energies on survival and not reproduction, which is why bleaching episodes that happen too soon after one another can have such disastrous consequences.

We scan the area yet again on a third dive with Victor, who is meant to document the spawning on video, and we bring back any promising-looking samples to CRIOBE for a second opinion from the science team. Underwater, a red ribbon, with a small white float that rises above the reef, is hung on each of the colonies sampled. Each float has a number and each sample is put in a bag with the corresponding number written on it by hand. We take 1, 2, 3, right up to 10. End of dive.

The samples we have brought back were gathered too far away from the Capsule for its saturation divers to do the job. Therefore, to achieve our objective, we must change our strategy, which will mean diving from the surface every night.

Evening comes and, while most of the team relax, Victor and I get our photo and video equipment ready, as well as our rebreathers. Laurent is coming with us today and we dive in at about 7.30pm.

Beneath the water the dive proceeds at a steady pace. We go from colony to colony, in a circular loop from 1 to 2 to 3… First we have had to get our bearings again. We had put the ribbons on in daylight. It is now pitch black. We must be careful that our lamps do not disturb the spawning. On approaching a colony we turn off all our lights but one. I take a few seconds to have a close look, then I take a photo, which allows me to zoom in on screen and see whether any eggs are visible; this is how we move from colony to colony, without lingering. There is no time to waste; spawning lasts just over ten minutes, so we must do our best not to miss it.

We emerge at midnight. Between returning to the surface and getting into bed there is about two hour's work (the journey back, rinsing and putting away our equipment, etc.), but we are well motivated! Spawning in a natural environment beyond the lagoons has never been documented in French Polynesia!

The next morning we go to CRIOBE so Laëtitia can confirm that the previous day's samples are indeed promising. The verdict: only one colony is about to spawn, sample number 5. During the day, a team of divers collects all the ribbons that are floating over the reef, except for number 5.

This second evening we focus on a single colony. Blanketed in complete darkness, this time our dive ticks by to a rhythm marked out by regular checks: I turn on my lamp, observe, take a photo, turn off my lamp and compare the photo to the one taken five minutes earlier. One… every… five… minutes. It's boring. We get cold, because we aren't moving. We dived at 7.30pm. We surface at midnight. Return to base, rinse, etc. It is 2am before I get to bed.

After eight long night dives waiting in the
darkness for the spawning, eggs finally appear
before being released into the ocean.

For the first time in French Polynesia, egg laying is documented on the outer reef. It lasts only a few seconds but is a unique spectacle for the divers who have totted up 30 hours underwater waiting to witness this phenomenon.

On the third evening the safety team help us to rig and dismantle our rebreathers, out of camaraderie and solidarity in carrying out this rather special mission. All the team members generously volunteer to take turns, night after night, to make our job easier. It's a real team effort! The support motivates us, despite the latest dive also proving to be a failure.

By the end of the fourth night we are starting to have some doubts. In the early hours of the morning we check to make sure that the CRIOBE specimen has not released its eggs. Because even though this branch has been disconnected from the rest of the colony it is still "programmed" and should spawn in the CRIOBE aquarium at exactly the same moment as when we should see it happen on the reef. We are reassured: spawning has not taken place yet.

While doing this check, however, we find that samples 3 and 5 may have been swapped, the writing on the pouches being confusing. So we take the piece of coral away with us to put it back onto its original colony, like a piece in a jigsaw puzzle. Verdict: we are in the wrong place. So we have been looking at the wrong colony for 16 hours! But the worst part of all is that now all the ribbons have been removed and it is dark, how will we find number 3? It's like searching for a needle in a haystack... in the dark!

We decide to try something, but to do it we have to return to the surface. Once there, we can access our dive history on our computers. Then we visualize the depth curve of that first night underwater, when the ten ribbons were still in place. Each flat line indicates a stationary position, corresponding to observing a colony for five minutes. We deduce that this colony must be at 17m (56ft). So we leave to do a transect, with no success. This time, I'm trying to do the entire route that we did that first night, using the landmarks that I had identified. I think I recognise one in the search area. I flip my fins a few times and scream into my rebreather's closed loop: "We've found number 3!" How can I be sure? Quite simply because the ribbon is still there, invisible from a distance but wrapped around the colony by the action of the current and the swell. Victor brings the sample. It fits together perfectly. What a relief! But we see no eggs. Might the colony have spawned already, while we were busy doing our underwater treasure hunt? Once again, we return, rinse, tidy away... and I break a toe in the process. I am furious.

On the sixth night we have rediscovered our motivation and optimism. We're sure we are in the right colony. Disappointment yet again. At 1am we surface, rinse, tidy... and I get bitten by a centipede. Am I the lame duck of the team?

The seventh night is another failure. Morale is at its lowest. But as we prepared to enter the water the following night we get a call on the radio to say that the sample at CRIOBE is starting to show signs of spawning. This news is just what was needed to put the smiles back on our faces and motivate us to dive. Immersion. We go straight to our colony and yes, the pink eggs are beginning to gather under the branches. Two hours later, the first eggs escape, rise a few centimetres and disappear, carried off by the current. The spawning slowly intensifies with a crackling sound, becoming really intense. I find it hard to believe that there can be so many eggs in such a small colony. Victor and I are ultra-focused. Thirty hours of diving to bring back images of this rare phenomenon, never before filmed or photographed in Polynesia: it is all about being on the spot. I take pictures and some video too. The adrenaline is at work. And then, within seconds, everything stops. That's it. As the culmination of all the team's collective efforts, we have just been privileged to witness a rare natural event. I can't wait to get back to the surface to break the news. Relief, pride, excitement and fatigue are all mixed together. But above all we know that, by confirming the day and time of spawning, we could help Laëtitia in her future research.

THE BENEFIT OF EXTENDED CONTINUOUS OBSERVATION IN MARINE BIOLOGY ON CAPSULE-TYPE SATURATION PROGRAMMES

DR LORENZO BRAMANTI

CNRS (National Centre for Scientific Research) Sorbonne University; LECOB (Benthic Ecogeochemistry Laboratory), Oceanological Observatory of Banyuls-sur-Mer

Capsule, a light underwater habitat for observing nature.

Ethology is the scientific study of animal behaviour, generally observed in the natural environment. The scientific roots of ethology lie in the work of Charles Darwin, as well as late 19th- and early 20th-century American and German ornithologists. The modern discipline of ethology is widely considered to have begun in the 1930s with the work of Dutch biologist Nikolaas Tinbergen and Austrian biologists Konrad Lorenz and Karl von Frisch, the three joint winners of the 1973 Nobel Prize in Physiology or Medicine.

The study of animal behaviour together with ecology, in what is called eco-ethology, is defined as the study of the relationship between the behaviour of animals and their environment. This discipline provides important insights into the responses of organisms to climate change and into the conservation of species.

Since the studies of Lorenz and Tinbergen, ethology has been primarily associated with the behaviour of terrestrial animals, especially large vertebrates. The classic ethologist, it is generally supposed, is a scientist who devotes long hours to field studies, in the forest or in the savannah, observing and describing the behaviour of primates, birds, wolves, deer etc. in their natural environment. Oddly enough, there is no similar character or specialty associated with the marine environment.

There are, of course, exceptions, such as scientists who study the behaviour of cephalopods and cetaceans, but these studies are mainly carried out in aquariums or based on observations by indirect means, such as acoustics.

So why are there no ethologists of undersea ecosystems? Is it because the behaviour of fish is not noteworthy? Quite the contrary! The behaviour of fish, and many other marine species, is complex, even fascinating; coupled with ecological data it can give important insights into the management and conservation of marine ecosystems. The real reason why no-one talks about undersea ethology is very simple: it is difficult to observe what goes on underwater for extended periods of time. Understanding the behaviour of animals

A meeting at CRIOBE, between Emmanuelle, Ghislain, Gilles Siu and David Lecchini, to establish the observation protocol for different fish species from the Capsule. Particular attention will be paid to behaviour, habits, sunrise and sunset phases and observations of predation or reproduction.

takes hours and days of observations in their natural habitat, but long-term access to the undersea environment is mainly limited by human physiology.

Over the past 50 years, technological developments have made it possible to extend immersion times. Open circuit diving thus enabled the first direct observations of the undersea environment, then the introduction of closed circuit systems extended the time spent underwater, allowing several hours of diving. Despite these efforts, even this is not sufficient for behavioural studies, which require observations lasting several days, so the development of underwater ethology has been limited.

Nowadays, the advent of advanced technologies such as undersea habitats, together with advances in underwater exploration such as saturation diving, allow *in situ* observation of fish populations, providing a modern insight into the behaviours and strategies of species whose cognitive capacities have long been underestimated and undervalued. Until today, however, underwater habitats and saturation diving technology required heavy equipment and fixed installations, limiting behavioural studies to a few fixed areas. This restricted range limits the potential of eco-ethological studies and thus the knowledge that they can provide. The "dream" of a marine behaviour ecologist is to be able to observe the environment continuously, for extended periods, and to be able to apply this protocol to different ecosystems.

Portable undersea habitat systems, such as the Capsule, which can be easily moved and set up in different ecosystems, represent the new frontier that will permit this type of study. Such habitats open up the door to a new kind of science: submarine eco-ethology, which will undoubtedly provide important results and give valuable insights into the management and conservation of marine ecosystems. ∎

EPILOGUE

WHEN NOTHING GOES ACCORDING TO PLAN

We were meant to reach South America, travel along its coast down the length of Chile and anchor in Ushuaia after sailing the Patagonian channels. Having crossed the borders of the Atlantic, Pacific and Antarctic Oceans, we should have explored the depths off the Antarctic Peninsula before returning to France. We had planned this trip in Concarneau, our base in Brittany, where our computers, smartphones and the internet mark out the virtual footprints of our future expeditions. Which they also did in Tahiti, where for eight months a small team prepared the WHY for this long voyage, in particular by changing our yacht's two engines.

But coronavirus decided otherwise... Like the rest of the planet, we adapted and waited. We postponed the start, until we had no choice but to cancel. It's always a great disappointment to abandon a project that you have fought so hard to put together, to witness the collapse of something that has taken so long to build. There is, however, always something to be learnt from an unexpected experience that will shape us differently, forcing us to venture into places we might not otherwise have explored.

Before bringing the WHY back to Concarneau and thus closing the loop, we returned to Polynesia for a final mission between January and April 2021. Because this was the only possible solution in the context of the pandemic, but also because DeepHope was already suggesting new questions to us, we returned to Tahiti, Moorea and Makatea for two and a half months, the duration of DeepHope II.

We left Polynesia by plane on 8th April 2021, the same day that a small crew raised anchor on the WHY. After four years and four months she returned to Concarneau, thus concluding the third Under The Pole expedition.

AND NOW? UNDER THE POLE IV – DEEPLIFE 2021–2030

"What to do next? Stop there, or continue the progress we have made with Under The Pole since 2008? And, in that case, how to follow it up? With what objective? To what goal? And with what ambition?"

We have been asking ourselves these fundamental questions many times a day in recent months, just as we have at every turning point of this life we have chosen, where passion, work, friendship and family life are intimately intermingled. Questions that we are also asking ourselves at the dawn of our forties, our middle age, which allows us to review our past achievements and bring the essence of our future projects into sharper focus. But in a time of growing youth protest for change, when public awareness is rising rapidly, the coronavirus crisis has been like an electric shock. In this very special year, the question of what our actions mean, the direction we should take has taken on a new seriousness, imbued with our collective responsibility for bringing about a sustainable society.

In the villages we visited in Greenland and across the Northwest Passage or in the archipelagos of French Polynesia, climate change is already a burning reality. Shorter sea ice seasons; grizzly bears moving into polar bears' hunting territory; entire villages being relocated on sleds because of coastal erosion and thawing permafrost, creating the first arctic climate refugees; coral bleaching; rising waters... there is no shortage of examples. What about the plastic pollution found everywhere, even in these remote refuges at the furthest corners of the world? At time of writing, the IPCC[1], in its latest report, confirms man's undeniable influence on the climate and sounds an umpteenth alarm bell. There is an urgent need to act and this requires collective and individual awareness.

[1]   The Intergovernmental Panel on Climate Change. Report, 9th August 2021.
To read the whole report, see: www.ipcc.ch/report/ar6/wg1/#FullReport

What can be done? What move should you make on this vast chessboard? How do you make yourself most useful? How can you contribute to humanity's greatest challenge?

We believe in the power of exploration, which is so typical of human beings, a characteristic that ceaselessly pushes them to look further, to answer the eternal question: "What lies beyond?" We also believe that this quest for knowledge is transcended when it is placed at the service of everyone, to serve the common good. It then brings the purpose that we seek for in our actions.

For 13 years we have led multiple exploratory undersea expeditions with Under The Pole. Some of them were pioneering and particularly notable for the rarity of the images brought back, others were noted for valuable scientific work done on them, or the technological innovations applied in an environment where Mankind can only exist on borrowed time: the Ocean.

These expeditions all focused on allowing plenty of time to explore environments that are little-known because they are so difficult to access – in polar zones for many years, tropical ones more recently – which made each of them an extraordinary experience. It was necessary to draw on exceptional resources to accomplish them. And while their goals have evolved over time, they were all based on a foundation of unshakable values: curiosity, team spirit, sharing, respect, sincerity and excellence. Beside all this, there is something unusual at the centre of UTP: our family. This unique feature, which seemed to be the only way we could lead our expeditions together while reconciling them with long-term family life, brings a personal touch that permeates the entire team and places human relations at the heart of the project. Certainly all these factors have combined to make UTP possible and allow it to continue to exist and inspire others.

This originality, combined with our passion, is a strength that presents itself as an opportunity chiming with the 2021–2030 United Nations Decade for Ocean Science for Sustainable Development. Under The Pole is taking part as a protagonist with special expertise, able to lead an ambitious global programme directed at increasing scientific knowledge of marine animal forests in the mesophotic zone, up to 200m (66oft) deep, parts of the ocean that are largely unknown although they play a fundamental role in their balance. We have called the programme DeepLife.

Today, our greatest motivation to act for the planet is our two boys, Robin and Tom. But apart from them, we have everyone's children to consider. Now more than ever we have a moral responsibility to work towards leaving them a sustainable world, a world of peace.

Emmanuelle Périé-Bardout & Ghislain Bardout
Founders & Directors of UNDER THE POLE

UTP
IN SHORT

UNDER THE POLE (UTP) is an underwater exploration programme combining scientific research, innovation and raising awareness to improve knowledge and preservation of the oceans. Since being set up in 2008 it has carried out three major programmes.

2010: UNDER THE POLE I -
DEEPSEA UNDER THE POLE BY ROLEX
A 45-day expedition combining travelling by ski and pulka with diving under the North Pole ice pack.

2014-2015: UNDER THE POLE II - DISCOVERY GREENLAND
21 months of underwater exploration in Greenland, with a wintering in the ice pack.

2017-2021: UNDER THE POLE III - TWILIGHT ZONE
4 scientific exploration expeditions, 30,000 nautical miles travelled with the WHY, 100 crew members, 25 scientists, 4 x 52-minute films
- **NORTHWEST PASSAGE 2017.** Research on natural fluorescence, bioluminescence and inventory of underwater biological diversitý.
- **DEEPHOPE 2018-2019.** 1,000 dives in 12 months of research on mesophotic corals in French Polynesia.
- **CAPSULE 2019.** Deployment of an innovative underwater observatory allowing continuous observations of the environment for several days.
- **DEEPHOPE II 2021.** Following the cancellation of the Antarctic mission due to COVID, return to Polynesia to further develop the DEEPHOPE programme.

2021-2030: UNDER THE POLE IV - DEEPLIFE
Ongoing programme

www.underthepole.org

The Under The Pole team
on the Capsule programme,
Moorea, 30th September 2019.

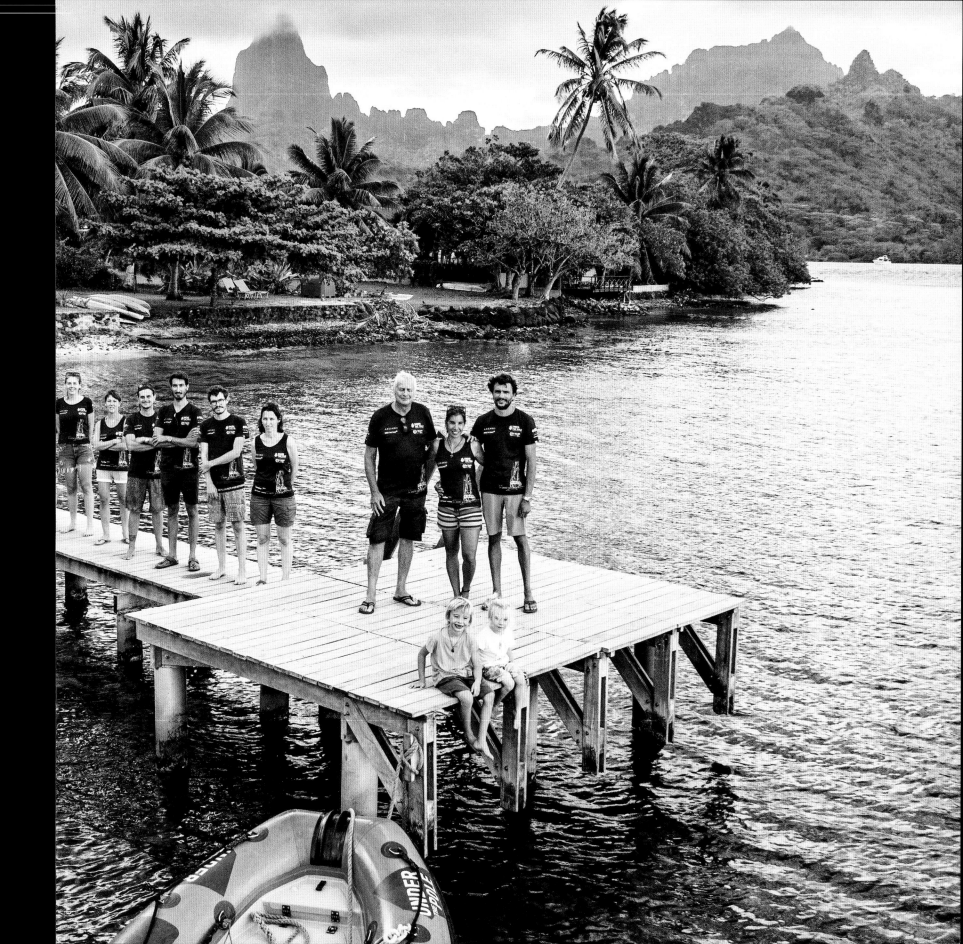

ROGUES' GALLERY

1. End of the day on the WHY. 2. Gildas, salmon fisherman and gold digger. 3. Manue emerges after three days in Capsule. 4. Thomas, happy photographer. 5. Camille and Tom's complicity. 6. Early initiation to the rebreather. 7. Nico, animal trainer. 8. The WHY and the team in Polynesian colours. 9. Ghislain, tooth puller. 10. Victor, muscular cameraman. 11. The Northwest team with friends Erik, Krystina and Frances. 12. Bilou, a sailor who stops at nothing. 13. Gilles, the man who wanted to live under the sea. 14. Manue, a captain who often steers with a child on her back. 15. Space station or underwater? 16. The student imitates the master, in electronics and fashion. 17. Everything will be fine. 18. Apolline, carefree cook. 19. Franck, devoted to science. 20. Reunion. 21. Sylvain, the Northwest's emblematic smile. 22. Miles, pet trumpet fish. 23. Julien, rain diver. 24. Friends on board the WHY: Julie Gautier, Guillaume Néry, Erwan Le Lann and Marion Courtois. 25. Dany, Nico and Ghislain, *tamure* dance specialists. 26. Kayak and Fukimi, love in Alaska. 27. Mental preparation: Tom at the end of the Northwest Passage. 28. Tic and Tac. 29. Sophie and Bilou in local colours. 30. When things get wild. 31. The most beautiful swing in the world.

1. The Gwenn ha Du flag, a bit of Brittany at the end of the world. 2. Tom, a dance fan. 3. Can't get wetter... 4. Diving total, 4,623 minutes! 5. Cautious peeler 6. Polynesian banquet. 7. To each his own. 8. Victor, well-equipped cameraman. 9. Floran, dedicated producer. 10. Manue and Erwan, passing the torch. 11. Robin, ready to dive. 12. Manue, a happy diver. 13. Charlotte, Laetitia and Manue, the "punch girl gang". 14. Two brothers. 15. In Raroia with Kiri and Mako. 16. Bernard, the human fish. 17. Robin and Bernard the squirrel, ready for the Northwest. 18. Tom, Capsule tour guide. 19. Big and little buddies. 20. Tired dive director, amused deputy. 21. When parents leave the kids with the team. 22. When their men leave for the Capsule. 23. When they leave for the Capsule. 24. Family photo. 25. Ready for love. 26. Where to next? 27. Worried chief of staff. 28. BBC film crew & Yo the captain. 29. Robin, future aquanaut? 30. Franck and Théo, photo and video team. 31. Guillaume, freediver and diver whisperer. 32. Scott, testing the Capsule, from design to reality.

THANKS

We firmly believe in the power of the group, the association of knowledge, the sharing of experiences and the strength of partnerships. The Northwest Passage, DeepHope and Capsule illustrate this magnificently and we would like to salute all those who have contributed to this success: the crew of course, but also the support teams in France for their commitment despite the 12-hour time difference, the scientists and their research institutes for their rigour and their passion for communication. We would like to thank all our partners, particularly Rolex (as part of its *Perpetual Planet* initiative), Azzaro, the Brittany Region as well as Bordier and Frisquet, without whom nothing would be possible. Above and beyond your financial support, your trust, your involvement and your values give real meaning to the word "partnership".

For supporting us in the successful execution of the DeepHope and Capsule programmes in French Polynesia, we especially thank the following institutions: Haut-Commissariat de la République en Polynésie française; Présidence de la Polynésie française; Assemblée de la Polynésie française; ministère de l'Économie verte et du Domaine; ministère de la Culture et de l'Environnement; Direction de l'Environnement de la Polynésie française; Action de l'État en Mer; Délégation de la Polynésie française à Paris; Direction de l'équipement et de la subdivision de Moorea; and the Océania association.

Thank to Laëtitia Hédouin, for her scientific management of the DeepHope program, her communicative passion and everything we shared together.

Thanks to François Gabart and Virginie Valentini for signing the foreword and being its first readers.

Thanks to the Académie de Rennes and in particular to David Guillerme and Christian Goubin for their support to our education programmes.

Thanks to Antoine Isambert for his enthusiasm and his determination to create the most beautiful book possible and to Guillaume Duprat for turning this idea into reality, within an extremely tight timeframe. Thanks to our proofreaders for their (very) great dedication: Edith Detemple, Raphaèle Dorniol, Laëtitia Hédouin and Franck Gazzola.

We could not have finished this book in time without the help of our respective families, who took care of Robin and Tom in Belle-Île-en-Mer and Concarneau while we worked. Thank you for the meals, the endless games of Mille Bornes ("1,000 milestones", a card game similar to the classic American game Touring), the fishing trips, the story readings, the ice cream... We are very lucky to have you. Thanks also, for your constant support since the beginning of Under The Pole, to: our parents: Marie-Noëlle and François Bardout, Edith Detemple, Guy and Odile Périé. Our brothers and sisters and their children: Thibaut, Paulina, Oscar and Armelle Bardout, Baptiste, Fatima and Paloma Bardout, Matthieu, Catherine, Juliette and Raphaël Bardout, Johanna and Scott Cameron. Thank you for letting us go, for being there even when oceans separate us, for sometimes joining us on the other side of the world, for maintaining such strong links with Robin and Tom.

Thank you to Marie-Noëlle and François Bardout, Roland Jourdain, Sophie Verceletto and Grib for taking care of Kayak while we were in Polynesia.

Thanks to our friends for always being there, by satellite phone or WhatsApp when we can't see each other physically and urgently need to talk.

Thanks to Franck who took most of the photos in this book but who also had the job of managing the entire image bank. What a long way we have come together since your arrival on the WHY in Greenland! A wink to Laure, who let you join us while fulfilling her own aspirations, and to the mischievous little Poppy, born during the DeepHope programme.

Thank you to the teams on board the WHY for working tirelessly towards the same goal, for not being satisfied with the minimum but for always doing your utmost to make the most of these expeditions. Thank you for taking ownership of these missions and their objectives and for being such fine people on board every day. Thank you for your kindness and laughter, the dives we made at the end of the world, the aperitifs, the shared discoveries. If we are the locomotive of Under The Pole, you are our engines, without which the train would go nowhere.

An affectionate thought for Kayak, who could not accompany us in Polynesia, but who became "Kayak – French Inuit Trans-Pacific Dog" in the Pacific.

Thanks to Robin and Tom for sharing our dreams while having dreams of their own.

Thank you to everyone, from near or far, who made all these expeditions possible. It's terribly difficult not to forget anyone! Most of you don't fit into one particular category but into two or three. We have done our best, but if we forgot someone, please forgive us, it must be from exhaustion!

Expedition team
Robin and Tom Bardout, Gildas Baronnet, Camille Breton, Johanna Cameron, Scott Cameron, Malo Castillon, Daniel Cron, Laurent Dieudonné, Paul Duncombe, Jérémy Fauchet, Aldo Ferrucci, Juliette Ferrucci, Franck Gazzola, Clément Genu, Lise Hascouet, Tommy Jégou, Gaël Lagarrigue, Stéphane Lameynardie, Julien Leblond, Clément Madelaine, Erwan Marivint, Thibaut Markocic, Martin Mellet, Rodolphe Merceron, Antoine Mittau, Nicolas Mollon, François Noël, Nicolas Paulme, Laura Peiganu, Romain Pete, Martin Plus, Yann Poupart, Sylvain Pujolle, Thomas Senk, Marta Sostres, Thomas Trapier, Kayak.

Land team
Baptiste Bardout, Anne-Claire Bihan-Poudec, Myrina Boulais, Gaëlle Bouttier-Guerive, Bastien Brionne, Tiphaine Champon, Grégoire Chéron, Cécile Cliquet, Stéphane Frémond, Luc Gesell, Angélique Honoré-Guilet, Frédéric Nasrinfar, Julien Pannetier, Jean Reneaume, Pol Robert, Karyn Roger, Tony Siegfriedt, Alexandre Soenen, Bruno Valentin. Trainees & Civic Service missions: Clément Albor, Benjamin Carette, Naea Grard-Dreneuc, Antoine Maltey, Laura Noël, Manuel Plus-Rios, Yohann Relat.

Film team
Benoit Carriau, Maxime Horlaville, Alec Magnan, Théo Moullec, Vincent Perazio, Kevin Peyrusse, Victor Rault, Floran Sax.

Other sailors on board the why
Ludovic Aglaor, Edouard-Marie Alikiagaleli, William Alikiagaleli, François Bardout, Mathilde Bessac-Desserteaux, Alexis Blanc, Bruno Casali, Nolwen De Carlan, Loïc Guenin, Armand De Jacquelot, Alice Leloup, Paul Marre, Aurélien Martin, Quentin Monégier, Laurent De Moroges, Julien Muller, Thomas Puiboube, Louise Ras, Maryama Seck.

Physiological and medical monitoring team
Jean-Éric Blatteau (HIA Sainte-Anne Toulon, Service de Santé des Armées), Emmanuel Dugrenot (Tek Diving SAS), Bernard Gardette (former scientific director of COMEX), Emmanuel Gouin, François Guerrero (Laboratoire ORPHY, université de Brest), Pierre Herrmann, Julien Hugon, Isabelle Jubert, Erwan L'Her (Laboratoire Latim, CHRU de Brest), Véronique Merour.

On-board scientific team
Frédéric Bertucci (CRIOBE), Chloé Brahmi (Université de la Polynésie Française), Cyril Gallut (MNHN), Laetitia Hédouin (CNRS-CRIOBE), Marcel Koken (CNRS - LABOCEA), Gonzalo Perez-Rosales (CRIOBE), Michel Pichon (Museum of Tropical Queensland), Héloise Rouzé (CRIOBE), Giles Siu (CRIOBE).

Scientific team on land
Cécile Berthe (CRIOBE), Pim Bongaerts (California Academy of Sciences), Lorenzo Bramanti (CNRS-LECOB), Benoît Espiau (CRIOBE), Pierre Galand (UMR8222, UPMC-CNRS), Yann Lacube (CRIOBE), David Lecchini (CRIOBE), Élodie Martinez (EIO, IRD), Monica Medina (Pennsylvania State University), Alexandre Merciere (CRIOBE), Marc Metian (IAEA), Aurélie Moya (ARC Centre of Excellence for Coral Reefs Studies), Jean-Baptiste Raina (University of Technology Sydney), Peter Swarzenski (IAEA), Greg Torda (ARC Centre of Excellence for Coral Reefs Studies).

For their support and valuable advice
Samuel Audrain, Pierre-André Auzias, Jean-Marc Bclin, Nicolas Buray, Éric Carret, Éric Clua, Christian Courtin-Clarins, Fanny Grossmann, Sophie & Khaled Hammal, Jean-Michel Huctin, Roland Jourdain, Michel Juvet, Annie Kerouedan, Églantine Larose, Yann Le Breton, Annaïg Leguen (CRIOBE), Alexandre & Mathilde Melun, Emmanuel Poisson-Quinton, Sophie Verceletto.

Long-time friends or those met along the way
Jorut & Joana, Ann Andreassen, The children and children's home team of Uummannaq, Adrien & Erwan (Kerguelen Islands), Frances Brann, Bob Cheetham, Erik de Jong, Uuinan Dreneuc, Louie Kamookak, Paaluk & Ane-Mette & Evona Kreutzmann, Julia Ogina, Jerry Puglik, Krystina Scheler.

Key partners

An expedition under the patronage of

 MINISTÈRE DE L'ENSEIGNEMENT SUPÉRIEUR, DE LA RECHERCHE ET DE L'INNOVATION
Liberté Égalité Fraternité

MINISTÈRE DE L'ÉDUCATION NATIONALE, DE LA JEUNESSE ET DES SPORTS
Liberté Égalité Fraternité

 MINISTÈRE DE LA TRANSITION ÉCOLOGIQUE
Liberté Égalité Fraternité

ACADÉMIE DE RENNES
Liberté Égalité Fraternité

Technical partners

 LESTRA   BAHCO   HIGHFIELD

 GUY COTTEN L'ABRI DU MARIN   HONDA

Institutional and scientific partners

 cnrs   CRIOBE

 UBO Université de Bretagne Occidentale  LABORATOIRE ORPHY OPTIMISATION DES REGULATIONS PHYSIOLOGIQUES   LABOCEA

 Muséum national d'Histoire naturelle   UPF UNIVERSITÉ DE LA POLYNÉSIE FRANÇAISE   OBSERVATOIRE DES REQUINS DE POLYNÉSIE

 THE UNIVERSITY OF QUEENSLAND AUSTRALIA gciQ Global Change Institute   JAMES COOK UNIVERSITY AUSTRALIA   ARC Centre of Excellence Coral Reef Studies

 MUSEUM OF TROPICAL QUEENSLAND  Ocean & Climate platform

Official suppliers

 Worldline   Capgemini engineering

FONDATION AIR LIQUIDE, EIF INNOVATION, MAUI JIM, SAFT, NIKON, PANASONIC, MC-TECHNOLOGIES, INTERSURGICAL, SCHOELLER ALLIBERT, CURTEC, PELI, SACHTLER, HI-NANO, AREMITI, AVIS, LÉA NATURE, KELDAN, JJ-CCR, BROWNING, SHEARWATER, NAUTICAM, SF-TECH, POMPES JAPY, HLB DIVE, KALYPSE, LUXFER, GRALMARINE, ABYSSNAUT, JW AUTOMARINE, DE-OX, NAUTIX, SQUID, NAVIONICS, MX TIMEZERO, GREAT CIRCLE, E-SAT, OPINEL, LANCELIN, PETZL, ENELOOP, EPIPHAN VIDEO, BRITT, SACHTLER, TERRE DE L'ÉLU, D-FIBRILLATEUR, SASSY, BOMBARD, POL ROGER, CIP GLÉNAN, MINOX, VALTAMER, COLORPIX, AIR TAHITI NUI, AIR TAHITI, JULBO, HOA, SUEX, DIESI, RACER, COLOPLAST, WESTERN DIGITAL, CRISTEC, CAT, PEDIAKID.

 EXPLORE.   SERVICE CIVIQUE

ÉCOLE PRATIQUE DES HAUTES ÉTUDES
UNIVERSITÉ DE PERPIGNAN VIA DOMITIA
AGENCE NATIONALE DE LA RECHERCHE
DÉLÉGATION À LA RECHERCHE DE LA POLYNÉSIE FRANÇAISE
INITIATIVE FRANÇAISE POUR LES RÉCIFS CORALLIENS IFRECOR

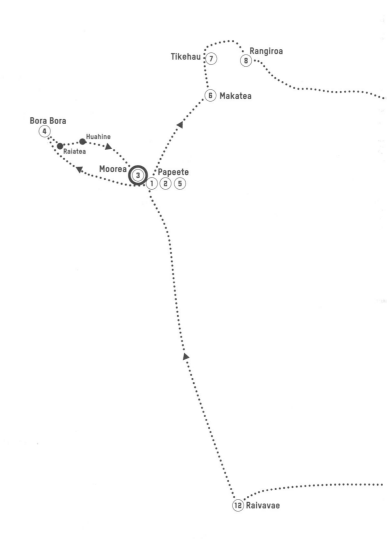

Tikehau ⑦   Rangiroa
                      ⑧

             ⑥ Makatea

Bora Bora
    ④
              Huahine
        Raiatea

        Moorea
              ③   Papeete
                  ① ② ⑤

⑫ Raivavae